Cécile Landau was a teenager during the sixties and has her own vivid memories of that era. Now resident in London, she has worked in book publishing since 1981 as a writer and editor. Her main interest in life is eating.

OPTIMA

GROWING UP IN THE SIXTIES

CÉCILE LANDAU

An OPTIMA book

First published in 1991 by
Macdonald Optima, a division of
Macdonald & Co. (Publishers) Ltd

A member of Maxwell Macmillan Pergamon Publishing Corporation

British Library Cataloguing in Publication Data

Landau, Cecile
    Growing up in the sixties.
    1. Great Britain. Social life, 1960–1969
    I. Title
    941.0856
    ISBN 0-356-15554-4

Macdonald & Co (Publishers) Ltd
Orbit House
1 New Fetter Lane
London EC4A 1AR

Typeset in Century Schoolbook
by Leaper & Gard Ltd, Bristol, England

Printed and bound in Great Britain by
The Guernsey Press Co. Ltd., Guernsey, Channel Islands.

CONTENTS

INTRODUCTION   vii

LAURA   1

JOAN   29

LEE   60

JULIA   90

ELIZABETH   111

SUSAN   128

ALEX   154

INTRODUCTION

'Why me?' replied most of the women I asked to talk about growing up in the 1960's. 'I led such a boring life,' 'I wasn't involved with anything that happened,' 'I was too young to really get into all that sixties stuff,' they said. So powerful is the media mythology of the sixties that even those who lived through them have come to believe that unless they were part of the 'swinging' scene, or had tuned in, turned on and dropped out, as the LSD guru Timothy Leary suggested, they were simply bystanders to the decade, untouched by its sweeping torrent of social change.

But by and large, the media exists to chronicle the 'highs' of life – the exciting, the scandalous, the controversial, the new – and there were certainly plenty of those around in the sixties. By contrast, the mundane routine of daily life is not newsworthy. Yet that routine is as much a part of peoples' concept of their lives, and thereby as much a part of history, as anything the newspapers have to tell us. In any case, routine and revolution can't be that easily separated. The changes or 'revolutions' brought by the sixties touched in some way or other upon every corner of our daily lives. Whether or not the seven women featured in this book went on the Pill and joined in the 'sexual revolution', or had their consciousnesses raised, or smoked dope, or 'dropped out', or became actively involved in liberal politics or Women's Lib, their attitudes and aspirations were set on a new course by the 'big' events of the decade. They grew up into a world in which little of the advice their mothers were able to give them seemed to have any relevance.

A growing awareness of her own femininity is usually the chief preoccupation of a young girl as she moves towards womanhood, and the seven women interviewed for this book were no exception. They may talk of many things, but their clearest memories are largely of clothes, boyfriends and the need to feel attractive. Career hopes and other ambitions are nearly always coloured by concern about how these will fit in with the probability of marriage and children. All this is nothing new, but grappling with the joys and confusions of female adolescence took on heightened definition in the sixties. It was a time when femininity was being rapidly and radically redefined. Suddenly there seemed to be more choices, and the definitions of 'right' and 'wrong' that had been passed on with so little modification for generation after generation became distinctly blurred.

It has been suggested that the new 'rules' of the sixties simply disguised the age-old tyrannies, that women were just as controlled by men, but in a different and less overt way. Perhaps the mini-skirt and the pressure towards Twiggy-like thinness made women just as much sex objects as had the Victorian bustle or the cone-shaped bras of the fifties. But this possibility doesn't seem to have entered the minds of any of my interviewees. Like most young women in any era, they focus on the fun and frivolity of fashion – and sixties fashion, from the mini to the maxi, certainly offered plenty of scope for that. And it should not be forgotten that women's clothing in the sixties, whatever else it may have expressed, spelt a move towards greater freedom. It was considerably more comfortable and less restrictive than it had been for centuries. Gone were the foundation garments and girdles that had restricted movement and squeezed and contorted the female form into an 'acceptable' shape. There was less formality, more variety at affordable prices and, as the decade grew to a close, a greater blurring of the outward differences between the sexes.

Concern was, however, expressed over the so-called 'sexual revolution'. Both Susan and Julia felt that the new permissiveness may have increased rather than decreased the pressure upon women to make themselves available for men. But most thought they had had greater freedom and more choices than their mothers or grandmothers ever did. Marriage was no longer the only acceptable route to sexual expression, and with the Pill – and, if necessary, legalised abortion – the pressure of assuming responsibility for the next generation could be postponed, or at least better planned and controlled. That left more time for personal development, for a career and other aspirations outside of the domestic circle, previously seen as the central focus of a woman's life.

But young women seeking new directions in the sixties were faced with a maze of confusion and little guidance. They were the *first* generation to be offered the possibility of a broader choice of lifestyle. Yet the careers advice still commonly being dished out by schools, even in the late sixties to the most academically able girls, was that although university and higher education were now fine, any subsequent career-plans should fit in with the duties of marriage and family. Nursing and teaching were generally seen as ideal occupations in this respect, once again casting women essentially in their age-old caring and nurturing role. In so many areas, young women, who sensed that things might not be so rigid in the future, had to be pioneers, and many lost heart. Women with enough power and authority to serve as examples and inspiration were a rarity, and access to most professional training was still severely limited. The seeds of the Women's Liberation Movement were only just being sown in the late sixties. It would take another decade of fighting and legislation for their campaign to begin to bear fruit.

However, much of sixties' thinking was essentially characterised by optimism, and those with the pioneering spirit, like Elizabeth, were buoyed along by it – in her case through the 'barriers' of both race and sex. Others, like Joan and Susan, found their outlet for broader experience outside the vocational sphere, through the widening opportunities for travel. Girls whose parents had never been outside England were jetting across the Atlantic or planning their annual holiday in France or Spain. Rising wages meant that many young people could think of moving into a flat of their own. If your parents didn't like your lifestyle, you could move out. Marriage no longer had to be the first step to independent living.

Above all, it was a great time to be young. The youth culture, born in the late fifties, boomed throughout the sixties. Youth was almost an object of veneration. Never before or since has so much commercial and artistic endeavour been aimed at the young. Never before had young people had so much spending power or so many opportunities to increase it. Jobs were in plentiful supply, and more and more youthful entrepreneurs were pushing themselves into positions of power and authority. Perhaps this youth-worship was a reflection of an unhealthy bias in sixties society, but it made it a glorious time to be growing up. For the young, anything and everything seemed possible.

LAURA

The year 1960 was my 11+ year and that was a real land-mark in my life. We'd been building up to it for ages. For years it had been impressed upon us at school how important the whole thing was. I felt that if I didn't get through this exam and do well, then I would never do anything with my life. To me it seemed like a major barrier that I had to get through, and then I'd be all right. Of course, I know now that's nonsense, because I did fail it and later I did a lot of other things that could have been considered disastrous, but I think I've come through all right. It's taken a long time, but I think I'm getting there.

Anyway, there it was, looming up in front of us, the 11+. We seemed to spend ages in class practising for it, taking mock exams and that kind of thing. What a boring business it all was. I couldn't really connect with it all, but I knew somehow that it was really really important and I was terribly nervous about the whole thing. It was as though that year at school was a barrier point. Up until then you could somehow make a bit of a mess of things and it didn't really change anything, but now things were serious. From now on you had to account for yourself. You know, that's what most of the sixties for me was all about. Mostly it wasn't about having a wonderful, free and wild time – like all that stuff you read now about the sixties. For me, it was about what I suppose being a teenager at any time is all about – growing up and taking charge of yourself, and I can remember finding that very hard. I don't think I was ever very happy for long in my teens.

We also moved to a new house in 1960. That was just before my 11+, in fact, which I don't think helped the situation very much. It was a much bigger house than we'd been used to. Also, it was almost out in the country – well, what you'd call suburbia, I suppose. And we had a garden, quite a large one, for the first time. My parents still live there. It's a lovely house. In fact, I really liked it, but it was miles from school and I wasn't good at making friends, and somehow the new house seemed to make things worse. I felt very isolated during that last year at my primary school. I always felt slightly out of it for all sorts of reasons, and one of them was definitely because my parents were obviously better off than the families of a lot of the other kids at school. I think some of the kids at school thought I was a bit of a softie and a bit stuck-up, because I'm quite shy and was rather quiet. I can tell you, moving to the kind of area where our new house was didn't help that image. The school was in an inner-city area – though it wasn't derelict or a slum – and there was I, suddenly living with the nobs in green-leafed suburbia. God, I got a lot of flak for that.

Later in the year, when I moved to a new school nearer to where we now lived, the problems I'd had with making friends at my old primary school soon stopped mattering as much. I was still shy, but I didn't seem to have the same problems fitting in at my new school. Let's face it, this is a pretty class-conscious country and it must have helped me that I was going to an almost totally middle-class school at last. It was all girls as well, which I think also eased things. Even at 10 and 11 there had already been this business of getting self-conscious and awkward with the opposite sex at my old school. Somehow, when it was all girls the whole atmosphere felt more relaxed and easier.

My parents were very lucky to get me into that school, because a lot of secondary modern schools then could be pretty large and many were quite rough. They were usually mixed too. All-girl secondary mods were a rarity, and this school was also small – so you got a lot of attention – and it was very strong on the academic side and on discipline too. It was very difficult to get into, I'd applied late, and was only just in their catchment area. Anyway, I did get in. I think there was a cancellation, and about a couple of weeks before I was due to start somewhere else, we got this phone call asking if I was still interested in a place. I was really pleased, because I suppose I thought it was a cut above the school I had been put down for. I was definitely a bit snobbish about things like that at the time, and going there made me feel less of a failure about the whole 11+ thing. Also, I knew people often did quite well from there, so I felt more confident about not making a complete mess of my life.

You'd think from the way I felt about the whole 11+ business and my worries about not messing things up and having to do OK, that my parents must have really pressurised me about getting on. But they didn't. They were pretty easy-going really. It was just that I'd seen them having to work really hard to get what they'd got and I felt it was important for me not to slip back and let them down. Neither of my parents had had much of an education. They'd started with nothing and built up their own business. It wasn't large and they weren't particularly rich, but they could now afford to give us a fairly cushy time, and I just got this feeling that it was important for me to make the most of all these benefits they'd given me. You know, I don't think they said anything when I didn't get into a grammar school, but getting into somewhere decent, despite failing the exam, made me feel much better.

Honestly, when I look back now I think I must have been crazy to put myself through such hell about school and doing well and that kind of thing. I can see now that all my parents cared about was me and my little sister being happy. They didn't mind what we did as long as it wasn't criminal, and we weren't having to waste our time slogging away in some boring old job for years and years just to pay the rent. They wanted us to feel interested and involved in what we did, but I don't think they had any preconceived notions of what we might do. Of course, they wanted us to do well at school, but we didn't have to be academic whizz-kids – though, actually, my little sister was. She's eighteen months younger than me, and she of course got into grammar school – in fact, she got a special scholarship place. Later she went to Oxford and she's now a doctor. I spent years thinking that she must be my parents' dream child and that I must be some kind of nightmare. I'm sure that had an enormous effect on the way I behaved throughout my teens and even into my twenties.

For the first year at my new school, I felt great. I made quite a few new friends, and for the first time I found it easy to bring people home. Most of us came from similar types of home, so it was just easier to feel comfortable with one another. The only thing I ever found embarrassing was my mother's taste in furniture. I don't think she has any sense of design, and I swear she's colour-blind. No one could do the kind of things she did to the decor of that house unless they were. The sixties were, I think, the first time she had any real money to spend on furniture and that kind of thing, and she certainly indulged. She said she didn't want a lot of old-fashioned hand-me-downs, so everything had to be the latest thing – which was really odd because her taste was quite old-fashioned in most other areas.

First she got this swish modern plasticy kitchen and quite a lot of gadgets. I can remember the arrival of our first automatic washing-machine. It was a Bendix and it had to be bolted to the floor, because it shook so much when it was spin-drying. The first time she used it, we all sat around and watched our clothes going around and around through the glass port-hole at the front. Machines like that were quite unusual in the early sixties. A lot of my friends' mothers still had top-loaders with electric mangles, though I can remember my best friend's mother getting a twin-tub. Clothes were still often dried on a rack, a long wooden thing that was hoisted up towards the ceiling with a rope and pulley system. Our house still had one of those when we moved in, but that wasn't right for my mother, so she had it pulled out. She also got rid of an old cast-iron range that was built-in over the kitchen fire. Too old-fashioned was what she thought. She can't believe that people pay a fortune now for those kind of features in a house, and that they're actually putting them back in. She thinks they're mad, though I now think she must have been a bit mad choosing a house with those kind of things in it in the first place if she hated them all so much. She spent so much money stripping things out of that house, and gradually painting nearly everywhere white with bits of pine and metal strips and bright-coloured plastic and knocking down the odd wall for the new open-plan effect. I fail to see why she bothered. If she had wanted an ultra-modern house, why didn't she and my father buy one in the first place instead of making that Edwardian pile of theirs look ridiculous? Thank God they've grown more conservative in their old age. The place looks quite reasonable now, though my mother's colour schemes are still pretty dreadful!

Strangely enough, many of my friends were in fact rather envious of my family's 'with-it' tastes in furnishings, so any embarrassment on my part at certain tacky touches was probably wasted. I wasn't totally anti the ultra-modern look – it was just my mother's seeming lack of discrimination at where and how to apply it that made me cringe. I can even remember choosing this rather cool, super-modern Scandinavian look for my bedroom/study when I was about 15. It certainly impressed my friends, but then I made sure my mother kept her hands off the colour scheme and that nothing was cheap and tacky. Do you remember those brightly coloured television sets? Well, we had to have one of those. My mother chose orange! It was ghastly. I kept telling her it didn't go with anything else in the room, but she didn't seem to mind. I left home soon after that, so the television must have arrived sometime in late 1967 or maybe early 1968.

I never knew why my father went along with all this. He's such a quiet man and he was much the same then, so I can't believe that some of my mother's more extreme ideas would have matched his taste. He wasn't at home a lot during my teens. He would be out early in the morning and not come home until pretty late. But when he was around, he spent a lot of time with us girls. He was always interested in what we did at school and who our friends were, and sometimes he took us out. He was really keen on the theatre and was always wanting to drag us along to something, which, when we were younger, we resisted strongly. I went to the local rep with him a couple of times when I was about 14. We saw some Noel Coward thing which I thought at the time was ridiculous, and some boring modern play that I can't even remember the name of now. Then he dragged my sister and I along on this trip to Stratford when I must have been about 15 or 16, and that was it. I saw David Warner in *Hamlet* and I was stunned. It was brilliant, absolutely brilliant. We stayed overnight in this B&B and I kept waking up and thinking about it all again and again. My sister thought I'd gone mad, but I just felt I'd never had such a wonderful experience in my whole life. The next day I went back and queued for returns for one of the Henry plays. I can't remember which one. It had Ian Holm in it, and it was also brilliant.

For quite a few years after that I was theatre-mad. I'd save up what money I had and would go to see all sorts. I'd even go down to Stratford and London on my own to see things. I mainly chose classical stuff. I don't remember ever going to places like the Royal Court, although I can remember going to the Hampstead Theatre Club and the King's Head in Islington a couple of times – but I think that was later on, probably in the early seventies when I was trying to get my life together after my awful marriage. I think theatre was one of the few things that I'm really glad I was around in the sixties for. It was a brilliant time for theatre in this country and I feel so lucky that I managed to catch some of it. I think I'm really very lucky in that respect. So many exciting things were going on. The Fringe was really growing and there were things like Peter Daubeny's World Theatre Season every year for several weeks at the Aldwych. There's nothing quite like it now, which I think is very, very sad.

I'm often surprised that I didn't want to do something in the theatre myself. I did do the props for this Little Theatre group in my last year at school, but I never took any of it very seriously. Probably somewhere I knew that I was just not the type for that kind of thing. I was very introverted. I still am in many ways. I'd really no clear idea of what I wanted to do, other than never have to work so hard as my parents had had to to get going. I definitely wanted an easier and more comfortable life than they had had to start out with. I sometimes had vague ideas, like when I was 12 I thought I might be a teacher, because it seemed like fun and just the right kind of job for a woman. Women's Lib hadn't hit me in those days. Then I decided that as I liked cooking, I could do something involved with that. My school wasn't very encouraging or helpful. They didn't seem to have any grand ambitions for their girls, and anyway at 12 or 13 they probably thought we were too young to be seriously considering such matters.

So in my early days at the secondary modern I just drifted through, vaguely grateful that I got into somewhere that could probably get me through enough O-levels not to have to end up working in Woolworth's. I also started to put some attention into my social life for the first time. I've already said that I found it easier at this new school to make friends and, now the dreaded 11+ was over, I probably felt relaxed enough for a while to think about having a good time. Perhaps it was all just part of becoming a teenager, but for a while – almost until I went to the grammar at 14 – I had quite a wild time. It didn't last all that long, no more than about eighteen months really, but it was probably the only time in the sixties when you could have said that I fitted in with anything to do with the whole media image of the times.

I had one particular friend at my new school and she must have had an enormous influence on me. Susie's family were very easy-going. I think her parents were quite young. Her mother had had her when she was only 18, and must have been no more than 29 when I first knew her. My parents were nearly 40, so there was a big difference in the atmosphere at Susie's compared to what it was like at home. Susie's mum used to like dancing, and music was always blaring out of the radio. I seem to remember that Radio Luxembourg was still the thing for pop music in those days. In her bedroom, Susie had this Dansette record player, which I lusted after. We used to lie around in there for hours, drooling over these records. They were all singles. We couldn't afford to buy LPs then, but you could stack about five or six singles at a time on her record player, so you weren't having to change records every few minutes. You could just lie back and really get into it.

Susie had this cousin who was a few years older than us, and who was crazy about Buddy Holly. He lent her some of his records and we used to play those a lot. She also had a bit of a thing about Paul Anka, and especially Elvis. In fact, Elvis was a really big thing with her. Even after the Beatles arrived, it was really still Elvis for her. I expect she still has a soft spot for him. But the Beatles did it for me. Until they arrived, I just used to listen to whatever Susie had to play, but when she got this Beatles record, that was it. *Twist and Shout*, I think it was, or it could have been *She Loves You*. I can't remember which came out first, but it certainly got to me in a big way. I just *had* to have my own Dansette then. The noise coming out of those machines must have been dreadful compared to what you can get now, but we thought it was wonderful and I was desperate to have one. I think they cost about £25 or £30, which seemed an awful lot of money to me. Maybe they were more, but I can remember going through what seemed like months working on my father to get him to give me one for a birthday present. Eventually he did. I don't think I've ever been so excited about any present before or since.

The Beatles must have dominated my life for about two years after that. I bought all their records, every single one, even the LPs, the lot. I always read *Beatles Monthly*. I think I even joined the fan club, which was really extreme for me, because I had a thing about not joining societies or clubs. I still have. And my room was plastered with pictures of them. I was madly in love with Paul. He was always my favourite. I never waivered in my affection. I used to spend a lot of time fantasising about them. When I wasn't actually listening to their music, I must have been thinking about them. What an obsession! Whenever I heard rumours that they might split up, I practically cried. I just couldn't imagine a time when the Beatles didn't exist. The weird thing is, I never went to any of their concerts. I think I was too young. I don't think I was even 13 when they first started making it big. Also, I felt that all those girls screaming themselves into hysterics were pretty silly. I felt I was above all that.

Susie was also getting into make-up at about this time. She didn't actually wear it to go out and I don't think she actually owned any, but we used to borrow some of her mother's and muck about with it in her room. I was hopeless with the stuff, but Susie was really quite good. Her mother did let her wear a bit sometimes when they had parties at their house. They had quite a few parties. Her parents would be there. They were really their parties, but Susie and her friends would be invited and some of the other kids in the street, and there would be lots of music and dancing.

I had my first encounters with boys at those parties. Susie was quite into boys, especially this guy who lived just down the road from her. He was very good-looking and I had a bit of a crush on him for a while, but generally I preferred dream men, like Paul McCartney, at that stage. Susie was more realistic. She liked the real thing. I think she was into a bit of kissing and mild groping, but I'm sure it never went further than that. We were barely 13 at the time. Once I went down to this chap's house with her after school and we were in his room with a couple of his friends listening to some records. Then suddenly the curtains were drawn and the lights went out and there was this great scramble on the bed. Susie thought it was great, all very funny, but I was terrified. I just wanted to go, so I started yelling and it stopped, and that was that. The boys weren't trying to do anything awful. It was just a bit of kissing and squeezing, and I did feel a bit embarrassed at making such a fuss. But for some reason, I'd got really scared for a few seconds. Also, I know part of it was feeling pretty stupid and ignorant, because I knew the others had done this kind of thing before and I was slightly worried about appearing to be a bit of a baby.

I had my first period after spending a Saturday morning round at Susie's with some of these boys. Nothing was going on, but I'd felt very peculiar and slightly sexy all morning. I kept staring at these boys and thinking perhaps it would be nice if something did happen on that occasion, but there was never any more of what I've just mentioned – at least, not while I was around. It was all very restrained, except that one of the boys was smoking and Susie kept trying to have a go. Her mother would have been furious if she'd come home and smelt smoke in the house. She was very strict about some things.

But anyway, I was feeling pretty odd and then I thought I felt a little damp, but for some reason I was too scared to go to the toilet and find out. I can remember sitting there being all grumpy and edgy and then rushing home at lunch-time. I must have run most of the way and gone straight to the loo, and there it was. I knew what I had to do, but for some reason I couldn't bring myself to tell my mother. It was practically evening before I did, and I had to keep using bits of loo paper instead of a pad. When I did get a pad, I hated it. I kept trying to use the loo paper instead, which was still awful and, of course, terribly messy, but I hated that lump between my legs. My mother was quite anti me using tampons. She said I'd have to have a baby first. But I ignored her, and eventually I just bought some and started using them. My parents never talked much about sex when I was growing up. They gave my sister and I this book when we were about 12, and said we could ask any questions we liked. We never did, of course. We would have been far too embarrassed for that. Everything I ever learnt, I found out for myself. It's a good job I was too shy and preoccupied with work to have much contact with boys for most of my teens. Though I think my comparative ignorance had something to do with the mess I got myself into later on.

Susie started going to a youth club and she wanted me to come, but for some reason I never did. I've no idea why, but I didn't. That was when she got really into clothes and she'd drag me along on these Saturday morning shopping trips. I'd always been a bit of a tomboy up till then, but I also started buying these skirts and pointed chisel-toed shoes, which were really fashionable at the time. This was 1962 or 1963, I think. My father thought these shoes were amazing. I don't think he entirely approved, but he was pleased to see me in a skirt for a change, and he let me wear nylons sometimes – like on special occasions such as our annual church visit at Christmas, or when relatives came to tea. I think he was proud to show the world what a wonderful, smart little lady he had produced. My usual jeans and jumpers didn't quite give that image. He even offered to buy me a handbag, which I refused.

I got quite into clothes for a little while. I don't remember wearing anything too exciting or daring. Skirts weren't all that short and skimpy at the beginning of the sixties anyway, and I hated make-up, so I never tried wearing any. As I've said, my parents were really pleased that I seemed to be moving away from my tomboy image. Then I changed schools. When I was nearly 14, I got a transfer to the grammar school. Although I hadn't worked particularly hard at the secondary mod, I'd somehow done pretty well. I'd never done that well academically before, and it came as quite a surprise to me at first, but it boosted my confidence and I never thought any more about it than that initially. The difference came when I got to the grammar. I felt slightly shocked to have got there and knew that if I didn't keep up to scratch then I might be thrown out, so I started taking my schoolwork more and more seriously. I became quite a swot, a bit of a bore really, and gradually I stopped spending so much time with Susie. I think I found her just more and more frivolous, which shows you what an uptight little thing I became.

I stopped taking any real interest in my appearance and in clothes. I practically stopped wearing skirts altogether, except for school. I thought they looked childish with socks and I'd always really hated nylons. I'd only worn them because I thought they looked more grown-up and because Susie did. There were no tights in those days, at least not ones you could easily afford, and I hated the suspenders digging into my legs. I spent all my time outside school in my jeans and jumpers again. My mother had real scenes with me whenever we were supposed to go anywhere half decent. I used to kick up such a fuss about wearing a skirt. I was ten times the tomboy I'd ever been before. Finally, she just gave up on me, and usually let me wear what I liked. I did have one smart trouser suit, and I turned out in that for most grand occasions. I don't think it ever drew full parental approval, but it passed. It was, in fact, a really trendy outfit, probably the most trendy thing I had at that stage. A friend of my mother's had made it for me from a Vogue pattern by Mary Quant, and it was in brown corduroy with a lighter colour edging. There was a matching peaked cap. Very trendy it was.

My interest in pop music lasted a little longer than my interest in clothes. I think it survived at least my first year at the grammar. I'd watched *Top of the Pops* from the very first programme, which I think was in 1963. Jimmy Saville was the presenter in those days. It had become a regular weekly spot for me, so I carried on watching for quite a long time after I stopped buying records. I think I bought my last pop records in 1965, and I gave away most of the records I already had to a children's home a couple of years later. Do you know I actually gave away a whole pile of Beatles originals? I wish I'd kept them, because I still like the Beatles, and I bet they'd be worth something now.

At the grammar, you could choose to have a weekly lesson in a musical instrument, so I chose the piano. The lessons were after school, but I didn't mind, and for a while I got really enthusiastic. I made terrific progress at first. It was when we got past the really easy beginning stages that I started getting stuck. It was really laziness and, besides, we were getting more and more homework, so I was finding it increasingly difficult to find enough time to practise in the evenings. My parents had bought me a piano especially, too. It was hardly touched after about the first eighteen months, and I felt terribly guilty about the whole thing. The piano lessons continued until I left school when I was 17, but the last few years were a bit of a dead loss. The only thing I got out of them was an interest in classical music, especially opera, which is something I doubt I would have come into contact with otherwise, considering how unmusical the rest of my family is.

If you were involved with music in any way at school, you always got roped in to help with the one cultural event of the school year – the annual concert or play. It was a bit of a philistine place, this school. We had no regular drama societies, music societies or art groups, or anything like that. If you wanted to do something like art or music for an O-level, you had to do it in the lunch-hour or in special after-school classes, as subjects like that weren't considered important enough to fit into the regular curriculum. So we only ever had one arty event a year, and that was usually a concert or play with the older girls taking the men's parts. I liked the concerts best, though I never had anything to do with the actual music side of them. I can't sing, and I don't think anyone was impressed with my keyboard skills. I'd usually help with organising things generally and I'd try to sing along off stage, but not too loudly in case I ruined the whole thing. They used to sing a lot of musical numbers and I got a real passion for American musicals of the fifties at about that time. In fact, after I'd stopped buying pop records, the only thing I ever bought until I left home was the odd LP of a musical – *South Pacific, Carousel, Oklahoma*. It was mainly Rodgers and Hammerstein stuff, and I used to shut myself up in my room and sing along to it. I was in a complete fantasy world.

I spent a lot of time on my own and a lot of time fantasising and day-dreaming after going to the grammar school. To my surprise, I did extremely well there. I thought I would just be mediocre at a place like that, but I wasn't. However, I never stopped worrying that I might slip back, so I just worked harder and harder until I never felt I had any time for socialising. That way, I got to have fewer and fewer friends and started spending most of my time on my own. It was stupid really, because I can't say being like that made me very happy. I was pretty miserable most of the time, and I know I secretly envied the girls who could have a good time and get their work done. My sister was like that, and I secretly hated her most of the time. Of course, I couldn't admit that I envied anyone, so I'd just pretend to despise them for being too frivolous and silly. As I've said, that's the main reason I drifted away from people like Susie. By now she was having what seemed to me like a really wild time, doing all the things that I now feel the sixties were all about – boyfriends, late-night parties, wearing these really sexy, skimpy clothes and loads of make-up. I still saw her occasionally, but I used to persuade myself that I'd never want to be like that because it was all pretty fickle and stupid, but it wasn't really. I think now it's exactly what I should have been doing at that age. It would have made me a lot saner and wiser later on.

By then my only really close friend was a girl called Margaret. She was a year older than me, but we had piano lessons together and that's how we met. She lived just around the corner from us, so I saw a lot of her in the holidays as well. I can't think now what she saw in an intense old swot like me, because she wasn't at all like that. She wasn't quite into such wild times as Susie, but I always remember her going to parties and buying these really short skirts that her mother used to gasp at. Margaret probably kept me sane. Without me I don't think I would have had a social life at all. Practically everything I did at the time, apart from working, I did with her.

I joined the Girl Guides, thanks to Margaret. She'd been in a Brownie pack and then she'd just drifted into the Guides. I don't think she was all that keen and hardly ever went, though she never got as far as leaving. Then I think her Guides started getting involved in these trips abroad and that must have made her slightly more enthusiastic. Anyway, that's when she persuaded me to join. It must have been to make the meetings she was supposed to attend in order to qualify for these foreign trips more bearable. I was 14 going on 15, and a bit old to start really, but somehow I got roped in. Meetings were as boring and ridiculous as Margaret had described. However, we did get two trips to Belgium and one to France out of it. I'd never been abroad before and Margaret had only ever been as far as the Channel Islands. My parents didn't take a holiday abroad until the mid-seventies. Until then, my mother had never been out of England, and I don't think that was at all unusual among people of her background.

I loved those trips. We had to wear our stupid uniforms most of the time, but we'd wear anything we fancied in the evenings and that was when we'd go round the local cafés and sometimes chat up the local boys. Those holidays were one of the few times I relaxed enough to get involved in things like that, and actually, I was never any good at the chatting-up bit – lack of practice, I suppose – but it didn't seem to matter. Maybe foreign girls were considered a special exotic attraction, no matter what. My clothes were fairly dowdy too compared to most of the others, but that didn't seem to put anyone off. Actually, there wasn't much pairing off. It was mainly group stuff, so I probably just blended in OK in the background. Some of the girls really knew what they were about. They may have looked pretty tame in their uniforms, but at night it all came out. One girl I remember had this silvery lurex mini-shift. It was one of those really short A-line dresses that were the in-thing at the time. This must have been 1966. She wore it with these matching silver tights, which must have cost a fortune because, as I've said, tights of any kind did at that time. I know that because my sister was always complaining about the cost of the things and how easily they tore. I don't think I bought more than two pairs before I was 18.

We also went camping with the Guides. Well, in fact, I only went once. That wasn't my idea of fun at all. It was cold, wet, and basically bloody awful. We had these really old-fashioned canvas bell-tents that you had to keep doing things to, like tying up the sides during the day for airing.

And the guy ropes needed adjusting all the time. It was all too much like hard work for me. I'm not the outward-bound type and, besides, no sane person would camp like that, even then. Margaret's family used to go camping quite a lot and they had this modern tent with zips and a special inner section. That never needed all the business the Guides' tents did. Margaret's family used Calor gas too. At Guide camp they mainly cooked over wood fires. We had to help gather the wood. I was never quite sure what was the right sort and what wasn't. In the end, Margaret and I took to using the odd firelighter.

Margaret had a touch of the tomboy in her too and, despite her equal aversion to Guide camp, she could be a bit of a sporty outdoor type. She was brilliant at athletics and I used to get to go with her and her family to all these meetings every summer. I think I had a better time at them than she did. She'd be kept pretty busy competing, while we'd get a chance to have really great picnics that her mother used to prepare. Margaret usually ended up with a few odd left-overs. We also went hiking in the summer holidays. That was Margaret's idea. She got hold of this book that described this series of walks around the local area. You were supposed to get a train or bus out to some real countryside and then follow the route given. Of course, that was the sensible way to do it, but we were crazy. We couldn't see how we could be real hikers if we took a bus part of the way, so on our first trip we set off from home on foot. It really was nuts. We lived in a fairly green suburban area, but it wasn't countryside. We ended up spending most of the day walking beside main roads. It was 4 o'clock before we reached the spot where the actual route described in the book began. We'd been walking since 10 o'clock and were exhausted. Eventually, we just gave up and ended up in a corner of this municipal park, lit our primus stove, heated up our tin of beans and sausages, and ate them with some bread and had tea from a thermos. If anybody bothered looking at us, they must have thought we were crazy. It was bloody ridiculous.

The next time, we decided that the book was right and

that the best place to start a country walk is in the country. Mind you, we also discovered what a stupid book it was. It would give directions like 'keeping the freshly ploughed field to your left, proceed along the blah, blah blah ...' Honestly, how did they know what time of year you would go on your hike. Just because a field was freshly ploughed when they passed it, it didn't mean it was going to be like that in six months' time when someone would be trying to follow their directions. No wonder we always got lost, though we were never seriously lost. We always found our way to somewhere interesting and the book was a great start. We saw a lot of the open countryside around our area like that. It was wonderful. We never did anything too strenuous or crazy, and we really did have a great time very cheaply. I don't think it would be safe now to let a 15- or 16-year-old girl go wandering off the way we did. Perhaps it wasn't any safer then, but our mothers never seemed bothered about it and we went to some pretty remote places.

As we got nearer and nearer to O-levels, I hardly went out at all. It was just work, work, work. I used to be up beyond midnight studying most evenings and then I'd be so tired that I'd fall asleep in class. And I must have started behaving a little oddly, because my mother eventually took me to the doctor. He told me to stop working so hard and put me on these pills to help calm me down and make me sleep better. I used to get so wound up with what I'd been working on the evening before that I couldn't sleep properly at night. I think it was wrong to give me pills, though. I may have needed a bit of talking to, but not pills. They didn't help either. I was still totally wound up and remained like that until the wretched exams were over. Now, I can't even imagine what I was so up-tight about. If I'd really sat down and thought about it sensibly it was obvious I was going to do well, or at least well enough for anything that mattered, but somehow I always had this overwhelming fear of failing. Perhaps it had something to do with my sister's brilliance. She always gave me an inferiority complex.

I don't know why Margaret bothered with me during that period. I practically stopped going round to see her, but she'd regularly pop round to our house. Of course, I was never free to go anywhere, though in the Christmas break just before mocks, I can remember her succeeding in dragging me along to a party. I hardly ever went to parties and I'd certainly never been to one like this. Obviously, this guy's parents were out, or away or somewhere. There was lots of beer around, mainly canned lager, and this constant really loud music, mainly the Beach Boys. But nobody was dancing. The idea seemed to be to get paired off as quickly as possible, find a corner or somewhere to perch, and start snogging. I'd never done that kind of thing. I was 16, but I don't think I'd even kissed a boy at that stage. I was terrified, especially as everybody else seemed so experienced, including Margaret, which for no good reason rather surprised me. I knew she wasn't as reclusive and naïve as me, but I had never thought she was that advanced.

Well, Margaret went off with this guy she seemed to know within seconds of our arriving and I just stood there petrified. I felt really out of it. I didn't know anyone, and I just couldn't imagine some guy fancying me enough to drag me off into a corner. Then the guy whose party it was came up, gave me a drink, and started talking. He was fairly good-looking and I kept thinking, 'What does he want? Someone like him can't be interested in a lump like me.' But he kept talking and I kept thinking, surely he's already got someone and she's going to come up at any minute. But nobody did, and eventually he just took my hand and we moved on to the edge of the sofa and that was that. He started kissing me. It was much nicer than I had expected, but all the time I was terrified I was doing it wrong and that he'd realise how ignorant I was. He probably could tell, but he didn't seem to mind. It seemed to go on for ages and I was definitely getting very worked up. I kept worrying that I might go too far and not be able to stop. I loved it. It was fabulous. I was totally and utterly in a complete state. I don't think I could have stopped myself even if I thought I ought to.

However, he obviously had much more control. Either that, or he was thirsty, because suddenly he got up and went to get some more drinks. He was gone for ages, so I just thought that that was that. Then he appeared again, minus drinks, and the whole business started again. Margaret rescued me the second time. She had to be home by midnight, so off we went. I tell you, I was in such a state. My first exposure to the opposite sex had left me in a complete shake. Margaret was totally composed, as though it was all routine to her, but I was smitten. I couldn't sleep at all that night. I kept dreaming about this guy and feeling all sexy and peculiar. It was wonderful and dreadful, all at the same time. I kept wondering if he might try and find out my phone number and perhaps ring me up, but he never did. That experience should have been a warning to me that I could get quite out of control as far as men were concerned, but at the time of course it wasn't. I wish now that I had indulged more as a teenager and become a little more blasé about sex. I could probably have put it in its proper place then. Instead, I became such a naïve little sucker. A few kisses and I'd practically be anybody's.

My next big passion, in fact my first real affair, happened that summer. Margaret had just left school and wanted to spend some time abroad before going to secretarial college. I'd just finished O-levels and was starting a completely new course in the sixth form in September, so for the first time in years I felt free just to go off and relax and enjoy myself. It was Margaret's idea to go to Spain. She'd arranged to do some language course out there, and after that she thought it would be great if I joined her to go youth hostelling or something. My parents were really keen on the idea, which quite surprised me. I thought they would say it was too dangerous, two girls on their own in a foreign country, but they didn't. The only stipulation was that I had to earn some of the money for it myself, so I got my first ever holiday job, cleaning at the local geriatric hospital.

I got to Spain by train and boat, because that was all I could afford. I don't think there were so many cheap charters in 1966. It was a terrible journey. I'd never been so far on my own before, and I kept having to remember not to get into empty carriages or those with just a few men in. I was so nervous that I don't think I spoke to anyone for most of the journey. I had to spend half a day in Paris alone. That's when I realised how hopeless my school French was. Then I got a couchette place down from Paris to Madrid, but I was too terrified to sleep. After that, the local Spanish train was dreadful. It was really over-crowded. People were standing everywhere, blocking the corridors. It was a nightmare getting to the loo, which was disgusting when you did get there, and you were likely to lose your place if you did get up to go. It was extremely hot too. I don't think there was any proper air-conditioning. When Margaret met me at the other end, I was filthy, tired, hungry and feeling sick. What a great start to a holiday!

Margaret wasn't staying in the youth hostel either. She'd moved into this cheap hotel, but wasn't sure how much longer we could stay there as she was getting the room for some special rate and more tourists were starting to arrive. I don't think it helped when I moved in. A week after I arrived we were told we would either have to pay more or go. Of course, we knew we would have to go, and I don't think it took Margaret more than a day to find a flat. It belonged to a couple of Americans that Margaret had met earlier. It was quite big and they said they weren't there all of the time, so we could have a room.

I'd met these American guys a couple of times before we moved in. I'd sort of guessed that Margaret was having a bit of a thing with one of them, and that was part of the reason why they let us move in. But even when Margaret told me that they didn't care whether we paid anything or not towards the room, I still didn't twig. Then we moved in and Margaret started spending most nights in Carl's room, and it became pretty obvious that I was expected to move in with Peter. He was actually very nice – blond and tanned and bit hippy-like. I did fancy him, but again I couldn't see what someone like him would see in someone like me. I had a very low opinion of myself then. Also, I was still a virgin, and the way I'd been brought up I somehow felt it must be wrong to sleep with someone before you were married. That didn't last long, I can tell you. It took me less than a week to fall into bed with Peter. The first night was a bit of a mess. I was very sore and it can't have been much fun for him, but he came back for more and that was it. I was hooked. I loved it. I also thought I was in love with him.

Carl hired this jeep and he and Margaret used to go off to all sorts of fascinating places. Sometimes Peter and I went along, but mostly we mooned around the beach and the bedroom. I'm amazed now that I never got pregnant, because I wasn't on the Pill and we never used anything. And what a waste! I spent a month out there and I saw practically nothing. I've still never been to places like Grenada or Seville. Apart from the climate, I could have been anywhere the way I was carrying on. I became quite clingy and possessive, and then very moody and tearful when I realised our month in Spain was coming to an end. Perhaps Peter thought I was becoming a bit of a pain, but he didn't say anything. He came to see us off at the station. I don't know now why Carl wasn't there, but I can remember that Margaret didn't seem to mind too much. There were lots of tears and Peter and I vowing eternal love, and then more tears and promises to write, etc., etc.

I was in the lower sixth when I got back, but somehow everything had changed. I just couldn't be bothered with school work any more. I just found it boring. All I wanted to do was to go out to the States and marry Peter. I didn't want to go to college, I didn't want a career and, for once, I didn't give a damn how well my sister was doing. I did less and less work and started getting terrible marks. I'd rush through homework, if I bothered to do it at all, then spend the time writing these long, gooey letters to Peter. He replied, as well – or at least for the first three months he did. Then just after Christmas the letters stopped and that was that. I continued writing a bit longer, but I never got any reply, so I stopped too. It's funny, but I don't think that by that stage I was too bothered. I can remember thinking at one point that I would be devastated if he didn't write but, when it actually happened, I wasn't. Maybe it was because I was starting to go out more and dressing up more and making myself look more attractive, so that I had more distractions and more confidence.

In the sixth form we could wear our own clothes, and there was definitely a kind of rivalry as to who looked the trendiest and who had the most clothes. I remember buying this quite short, bright orange A-line dress. It had this enormous brass zip right down the front. If you pulled the zip right down, the whole dress would have fallen off. And in summer I bought this sleeveless job in bright pink, orange and purple stripes. That was really really short, much shorter than anything I had ever worn before. It was positively dangerous. I also got my hair cut in a sort of Vidal Sassoon geometric cut, which was in fact getting a bit *passé* even then. My mother's hairdresser did it, and she was definitely always a few years out of date. It was also a pain to keep. Every time you washed it you had to sellotape it down while it was drying so that it would lie correctly. I soon gave that up and started growing it again. I didn't have my hair cut properly again until 1969. Then I went to Vidal Sassoon in London and got one of those cuts where it was all short on top with these long tendrils coming down the side.

My exam results at the end of lower sixth were terrible, so I just told my parents I wasn't going back. I don't think they took me seriously at first. Then it sunk in when I got this office job in town. My father didn't say too much. Perhaps he thought it would blow over and I would go to the local college in the September. My mother was a different story though. She and I had some fairly major rows that summer and, to make matters worse, I was stupid enough to tell her all about Peter in Spain the year before. Eventually, things got so bad I left home. I don't think I really intended to go for good. A girl I'd been quite friendly with in the fifth form was now living in Cornwall with her family. We used to write quite regularly and, when I told her things were bad at home, she suggested I came down for a bit.

I stayed with her family for nearly a month, but by that time I began to feel a bit uneasy about outstaying my welcome. I had this part-time job in a local hotel working in the bar and they offered me live-in accommodation, so I moved. That's how I met my first husband, Keith. He was on some posting down there and used to come into the hotel for a drink. One night when I was on the late shift and the bar was practically empty, we got chatting. I never really thought about him fancying me. He was quite a bit older than me. I just thought he was being nice. Then he asked me out to dinner. That was a couple of nights later, and I was surprised when he turned up and even more surprised that we got on quite well. He took me out a couple of times after that. I think I was lonely and he was good company, but I wasn't anything more than mildly attracted to him at that stage.

We really got together when I lost my job at the hotel. He was renting this house and had a spare room. It was the Peter and Spain syndrome all over again. First I moved into the spare room, then into his room, and the next thing I was madly in love. This was it – the real thing. I don't think I stopped to notice that we had practically nothing in common. He was protective and kind and loving, and I thought it was great. I was totally blinkered. All I could think about was us, the relationship, and not what I wanted from the rest of life. I stayed at home and took care of the house and the shopping and he provided the money. I was playing at being the little housewife, and I must have been very convincing because that was exactly the kind of woman that suited Keith and he was taken in by it. I think we probably both were. When I got pregnant a couple of months later, I took it for granted we would get married. I never thought about having an abortion. Being Keith's wife and a mother just seemed the most natural thing in the world at the time.

I took Keith home to meet my parents. They must have been horrified. They didn't say much, but I could tell they didn't look very happy. I think up until then they had hoped I would eventually come home, go to the local college, and at least get some A-levels. My father had always been keen on his daughters having enough educ-ation to be independent and earn their own living, and here was I putting myself in a position where I was totally dependent on a man – and a man who obviously liked it that way as well. Only my mother and sister came to the wedding. We got married in the local register office down in Cornwall. My father's name was on the present they gave me, but he never really acknowledged Keith as my husband. Even now, he never mentions my first marriage – despite the fact that he adores his grandson.

I started waking up to reality soon after Tom was born. We'd just moved to London and Keith was out all day and often home late. I felt trapped at home with a small baby. I wasn't yet 19 and most of the women I met in a similar position were quite a bit older than me, or at least they seemed it. Sometimes I had to play the executive wife and entertain Keith's business colleagues. In some ways, I was OK at that. I'd always been a good cook, but I felt like a Martian at most of those dinners. I had absolutely nothing in common with any of the people Keith ever brought home and he seemed to fit perfectly into that world. That's when I began questioning what we had in common. Don't get me wrong. On the surface, nothing much had changed. Keith was still very loving and kind and generous. I was very comfortable and had no money worries, but I was bored. Then my sister turned up for a weekend. I don't know what she thought of the whole set-up, but she insisted on dragging me along to this party, leaving Keith at home with Tom. I think Keith thought it was outrageous, me leaving him with the baby and going out without him, but I don't think he dared say anything in front of my sister.

I met a girl I'd known vaguely at school at this party

and we exchanged addresses. We didn't get in until 2 o'clock and Keith sulked for the rest of the weekend. My sister pretended she didn't notice, but I think she did. After that, things just got worse and worse between Keith and I. We still sort of got on as before, but there was less and less real contact. He must have been aware of what was happening, but he never said anything. He just got more and more involved with work and I eventually got in touch with this girl I'd met at the party. It took me ages to get round to it, and I felt a bit daft ringing her up at first as I couldn't imagine her wanting to spend time with some frumpy old housewife. I'd known her mainly because we had been part of a small group at school doing art. She was now at art school and suggested I might like to come along to one of the evening life classes and perhaps to go for a drink afterwards. To me it sounded like a crazy idea at first. I hadn't drawn for years, but I was desperate to get out and meet people my own age, so I found a babysitter and went. The first time I'd planned to get out before Keith came home, but for some reason he was early. I hadn't told him about the babysitter or what I was doing and he was furious. We had our first major row. I think that's when I first knew for certain I was going to leave him.

Soon after that our sex life became practically non-existent. I'm sure I only gave in to him occasionally because I felt sorry for him. Then it did become non-existent, and stayed like that until I finally had the guts to leave about eighteen months later. I was having an affair by then, but that wasn't the reason I left. It just helped spur me on. I'd starting going to evening classes at the art school twice a week and was really getting into it – not just the work, but the whole lifestyle. We'd usually go for a drink and sometimes a curry or a Greek meal in Soho afterwards. I loved it. It was about the only time I felt relaxed, felt as if I could be myself. The guy I had the affair with was one of the tutors, though he was younger than Keith. He was only in his mid-twenties and lived in this squat in south London. I'd sometimes meet him there in the afternoons and we would spend the whole time making love and talking. I used to take the baby with me. Gavin adored Tom.

It's funny in a way, using an expression like 'making love', because I was never under any illusion about being in love with Gavin, which made a change from my past record with Keith and Peter. It was just about having a good time and being friendly – very hippy-dippy and late sixties, I suppose. He was a great guy. He introduced me to a completely new way of life. There were loads of squatters' communities in London then – I don't know whether they still exist – and I made so many new friends, some of whom I'm still close to. What a time that was! In the morning I'd spin my way through my housewifely duties, dress Tom, and off we'd go to spend the afternoon leading this hippy, commune-style existence in a south London squat, then it would be back to middle-class executive suburbia to cook my husband's supper by 6 o'clock. Sometimes the thought of what I was doing made me very sad and depressed. At other times, I used to think it was all hilarious, but of course it couldn't go on for ever. There had to be a breaking point and that happened through Sue.

She was about three years older than me and was squatting with her son near Gavin. She was on the dole, but sometimes sold crafts and other bits and pieces at a weekend market. We got on really well and I started helping her on the stall. Keith hated that because it took me away from him at the weekend. He would never have approved of someone like Sue, so I never bothered introducing them, though he knew where I was going. I couldn't be bothered hiding that from him. Then Sue got this chance of a house of her own. It was a squat, but it was really nice. She knew about my situation with Keith and one day she said, 'Why don't you leave? You might as well do it now, as you could move into the house with me.' So that was that. I did. As I said, I'd known for a long time I was going to leave Keith. I'd been waiting for the right opportunity and this was obviously it. I'd needed some-

where definite to go because of the baby, and here it was.
It never bothered me that it was a squat. Actually, it was
more like short-term housing. The council knew we were
there and we paid all our bills and things. We basically
had permission to stay until they decided what they were
going to do with the properties.

I felt I had to tell Keith I was going, though I'll never
know how I got the guts together to do it. In fact, he made
it quite easy in the end. He hardly said anything when I
told him, and on the day I left he just went off to work as
usual. He could have taken the day off, but I don't think
he wanted to be in the house while I was packing. I don't
remember him saying goodbye to Tom or even looking at
him. That upset me at the time, but later I realised that
losing Tom must have been what hurt him the most. He
simply gave me a peck on the cheek and said goodbye. I
must say I admired him for taking it so well. He gave me
some money as well and told me to ask for more when I
needed it. I never saw Keith again after that. Our only
contact was by letter. I hadn't expected it to be quite that
final but it was.

For the first year Keith helped me out with money, but
then that stopped and, as I was doing OK by then, I didn't
bother trying for maintenance. For a while he also saw
Tom regularly, but he wouldn't come round to the squat to
collect him or have me bring him to the house. Tom had to
be taken to Keith's mother's place and she'd bring him
back. She was very nice. In fact, I think we got on better
after I left Keith than before. Then Keith went abroad to
work and for a couple of years he wrote the odd letter and
sent Tom presents, but eventually that stopped. Tom
must have been 6 when we last heard. I've tried to get in
touch again for Tom's sake, but there's been no joy. I
don't really care any more. In fact, not having Keith
around has made things much easier for me and Tom
never mentions his real father. I'm sure he can't really
remember him, though I sometimes think he must be
curious and a bit sad. Sometimes I get angry with Keith
for kind of abandoning his son, and at other times I think

the whole business must have hurt him so much that I understand what he's done. Though I'll always go on hoping that one day he'll ring Tom up.

So much of my life just fell into place after Keith. Sue and I progressed from the market stall to our own shop, selling crafts and odd bits of bric-à-brac. Some of it was just plain junk, but attractive junk, and people bought it. There was quite a vogue for that kind of thing at the beginning of the seventies. When Sue left, I had enough contacts to continue on my own. The business just grew from there. I've never had to go back to working for someone else. In a way, I don't regret Keith and getting married so young, because I'm sure I would never have ended up doing something like that if I'd taken my A-levels and gone to college. I'm sure I've had a more interesting life than I would have had if I'd done that.

It's funny in a way that I've ended up running a business, after vowing never to do it because of seeing how hard it was for my parents in the beginning. But I've been lucky. I've never had to struggle the way they did when starting out. Mind you, I don't think now I'd advise anyone to do what I did. I always think of myself as having had little or nothing to do with sixties culture. Even in the squat, I never got into dope or anything like that, but the kind of atmosphere that was created in the sixties, particularly towards the end, made it a lot easier to leave Keith than I think it would have been, say, ten or even five years earlier. And it made getting into business and making enough to live on easier too. I can't imagine starting in the way I did now, especially with a small baby in tow. The whole thing would just be ridiculous.

JOAN

I was 10 in 1960 and I can't remember that much about it. I remember being 11 because I was just starting a new school and meeting all these new people. I went to an all-girls grammar run by nuns, the typical sort of scene that it was then. You couldn't do this. You couldn't do that. You weren't even allowed out of the school grounds until you were 14. That is, you weren't allowed out during school hours. It wasn't boarding school – or rather, it was – but I was just a day pupil on a scholarship, one of the plebs who went home to Mum in the evening. There was no socialising at school and you weren't allowed to talk to boys. Of course, there weren't any in the school, but if you were seen talking to a boy, say at the bus stop or in town, you were punished in some way and a letter would be sent to your mum saying you were talking to boys. The boy involved could even be your brother, but you still weren't allowed to talk to him.

There was a boys' school not far away, an all-boys grammar run by the Jesuits. I think once a year the seniors from the boys' school were brought over to meet the seniors from our school, but we weren't allowed to look at them as they came in. As they walked into the school, we all had to turn our heads and let them just get through. Oh it was really archaic. I remember my older sister saying once that they'd all been given a talk in which they were told that if a boy ever wanted you to sit on his lap, you had to put newspapers between you.

I have two sisters and a brother. We all got scholarships. My sisters and I went to the convent and my brother went to this Jesuit boys' school. Mind you, we were the only family in our village that did go to schools like that. We lived in a tiny mining village in the North-East near Sunderland. There weren't many people. Nobody had cars and material things. Everyone was very poor. My parents had no money at all, so I think they were pleased when we got scholarships to schools like that. I don't remember them pushing us very hard, but I think they wanted us to be able to get good jobs, and everybody knew that if you were going to get a job that wasn't in a factory, you had to go to the grammars. There was no way you were going to do that otherwise.

My parents had never had such opportunities. Among their generation, most people had left school at 14 or 15. My dad had always worked in the pits and I think my mother used to be on the buses or at a sweet factory or something like that before she got married. Once a woman got married, she didn't work. A couple of our women neighbours used to work and they were looked down on. It was scandalous. They were considered terrible people, you know, bad mothers. It was that sort of community, a funny little place. Everybody knew everybody else.

The only hope of escape was to get into one of the grammar schools, then into a good job in the town. But when you are 11, you don't appreciate that. You are missing your friends. You don't really want to go – and then when you get to one of these schools, there are all these paying pupils with all the right clothes and uniform, while you're having to wear stuff that your mother's made or you're going to the nuns to get hand-outs and freebies. Home-made things never looked like the proper stuff, and in the end my mother bought most of my school uniform. She bought it so that I would grow into it. My tunic was nearly down to my ankles. I was quite tall when I was 11 but I didn't grow much after that, so it was always too large. I looked a right twit.

I also used to think that some of the subjects they taught at this school were stupid. For instance, you could learn Spanish. I couldn't understand why I should want to learn to speak Spanish. I'd never even been as far as Newcastle! To me, it just seemed ridiculous. Then they really got into things like maths. Well, I couldn't figure that out either. As long as I could add up the sums at the shops, I didn't see why I needed maths. I just thought it was all ridiculous and I wasn't really keen on the subjects

I was being taught anyway. Instead, I was always doodling. I just used to draw. I was always being given notes to take home saying I wasn't doing my homework and things like that, while my older sister, who was also at the school, was a real goody-two-shoes. She did everything that she was told to. She always looked neat and tidy, while I had my collar up and tie all loose, just doodling away.

It was a bit of a culture shock going to that school. A lot of the girls there came from families who went abroad and stuff like that and went on trains. I'd never even been on a train when I was 11. There was very little mixing. The paying girls would speak to you, but then they went off their own way. I don't think they ever really mingled. It was the same at the boys' school. But you didn't feel like a second-class citizen. I've never let anyone make me feel like that. The nuns were always really nice. If they knew a family was in difficulties or really poor, then they did genuinely try to help. I know nuns have got a name for being ogres, which a couple of them were, but most of them were very nice. They did try to help and not make an issue of it all. It was these other girls that were the problem. If you did get friendly and go out with any of the ones with money, you felt out of place because they always had new clothes which you could never afford. Once I did go to stay with a girl who was well-off. Her family had a lovely place. She had a party there and I'd never seen a house like it. Now it's what I'd consider a typical semi, but then I thought it was so big, a sort of mansion.

My parents never let us have parties like that, but we did have one once when my mother was away. My mum had gone away to the caravan – that's what they did for their week's holiday – and I kept saying that I didn't want to go. I was 15 and I didn't want to go off to a caravan, so she said she was going off on her own. I think my brother also stayed behind so she just took my younger sister. My elder sister must have been in London by then. Anyway, as soon as she was gone, I organised a party, the only party we ever had at our house at that time. I had to bribe my brother not to tell. We got all the booze in and everything and moved all the furniture out of the way. Then at about 1 o'clock in the morning the police turned up looking for somebody. We saw them coming up the path, so what the fellas did was they shoved all the beer bottles under the settee. We thought that you weren't allowed to drink at our age, even indoors, so we didn't want the police to see the beer. The fellas were hiding bottles everywhere and beer got spilled all over the place. Afterwards we couldn't get rid of the smell, and all the police had come for was to get one of the girls. She'd told her mother she was going to a youth club and it was a bit late, so her mother had got them to look for her. That party went on until about 3 a.m.

Entertainment in our house actually centred around books and music. We always had our own books and my dad used to play in brass bands. The whole family, his family that is, used to be in the local brass band and my mother's family played in dance bands. We kids can't play anything, but they were always playing and singing and stuff like that. We didn't have television until I was about 10 years old. Before that, if we wanted to watch telly we used to knock on a neighbour's door and ask if we could watch theirs. We listened to a Rediffusion wireless until my mum and dad won the jackpot at bingo and bought a transistor radio. It was around about the time when Radio Caroline first came on that we got that transistor. Before that, there had just been the normal BBC and Luxembourg.

Then came the major revolution – The Beatles. That was it. A lot of my class immediately latched on to The Beatles. We used to go down to the record shop. This was, I think, in 1962, and we got them with the first one, *Love Me Do*. I started to get really into pop music. I had a friend in South Shields and we'd spend most of the summer holidays in each other's houses, playing her tape-recorder. She used to tape all sorts of records and we'd listen to them in her room. There was a big fairground near South Shields and, when we weren't listening to music, we'd spend all our time there. We used to spend

half a day just on the waltzer. Then we started going to the
youth clubs. That must have been when we were about 13
or 14. These youth clubs were all run by the churches and
some of the parents would drive around in a mini-bus,
pick everybody up and take them to the nearest one, and
then pick them up again later to take them home. So we
started going to the clubs. Obviously, they played music
there. It was mainly rock 'n' roll or stuff like rock 'n' roll.
We used to stand around and see what was going on. That
was the social life.

I had this pair of white kid stilettoes that came out only
for youth club on Sundays. I got them from the catalogue
and I was buying them over the usual twenty weeks, or
however many weeks it was you could have. Anyway, this
pair of white kid stilettoes had square toes, which were
quite the thing then, and I put that white stuff on them to
keep them clean. Ooh, I thought they were lovely! I was
only 14 and I could barely walk in them. That's why they
only came out for youth club on Sundays. It was too much
to wear them more than that. I used to totter around in
them. And I'd wear stockings. I think you could just get
tights, but they were very expensive. I tried to get those
stay-ups with the elastic at the top, but they cut you in
two. 'Stranglers', that's what they were! And of course I
was getting into make-up. I was sticking on false eyelashes.
It drove my mother crazy. She'd look at me and say, 'You're
not going out like that!'

I started getting interested in clothes too. I'd never had
many clothes. We couldn't afford them and also, with a
school uniform during the week, we didn't need them. My
mother would make a lot of our clothes and you'd have one
dress, maybe two, that you could change into from your
school uniform. She was also a smashing knitter. Our
shoes came from the catalogue. From when I was about
12, I had to buy all my own clothes and things. I don't
think it was anything nasty. It was a fairly normal occur-
rence in most families I knew. It was just that they couldn't
afford them. If I bought the material or whatever, my
mother would make stuff, but she couldn't afford to buy it

herself. I used to babysit to get money for clothes. I did about three babysitting jobs a week. Then I got Saturday jobs down in the town. I worked in Woolworth's, at first on the records. They weren't proper records, just special cheap cover versions. They had the most awful covers. However, I was taken off the records because I was playing them all day long at high volume. I was put on artificial flowers and then on ice creams, which wasn't quite what I wanted but I didn't really care. I just needed a job. All my friends had Saturday jobs.

But my interest in fashion didn't really last that long. I must have been about 12 or 13 when I got into it, along with all the other girls, and by the time I was about 16 or 17 I'd lost interest. I gave up quickly. It wasn't a major experience. I've never looked trendy. I've always been the wrong shape. My sisters could get things quite easily, but the average height was estimated at around 5'4" then – and when you're very short like me it's not like that. I mean, most of my minis were only just above the knee. If I bought a mini that's where it came, and I was damned if I was going to shorten it. If my mother didn't shorten it, I didn't. So I found it really difficult to follow fashion, and in the end I think I just gave up. Also, if you wanted something really interesting, you had to make it. All bought dresses were the same. It was horrible. You'd go off to a dance and there'd be six of you, all in the same dress. It was awful. You could only have fairly decent clothes if you made them, but it was always difficult getting the right material, and anyway I couldn't sew and my mum would have refused to make anything like a real bum freezer. In the end, I just didn't bother. I don't think I've followed fashion since.

In fact, I didn't really see that much fashion. The only magazines I used to buy were *Beatles Monthly* and *New Musical Express*. There wasn't much fashion in either of those and it took about six months or more for anything fashionable to reach the North-East. London was well into minis, it was splashed everywhere that this revolution in dress had taken place, before any of it reached us. I remember still wearing tight skirts and stilettoes in the mid-sixties and trying to hobble on to the bus and things. It was a long time before minis made it up North. In fact, I think it was about 1966 or 1967 before they reached our village. They may have worn them in Newcastle before that, but not in Sunderland.

I only actually went to Newcastle once. I went with my friend from South Shields. We went on a train. It was quite exciting. Before that, the farthest I'd ever been was to South Shields and on a day trip to Holy Island with the school. I don't think I'd even been on a train before then. It was considered very expensive. My dad used to give me about a pound pocket money for the whole summer holiday. That would have to last me six weeks, for whatever I wanted to do. I know things were a lot cheaper then, but I couldn't just go home and say, 'I've run out of money. Can I have some more please?' They didn't have it. If my dad had had it, he'd have given it to me, but they just didn't have that sort of money. So I had to eke out what I had, and going on a train somewhere wasn't really a priority.

But we did take the train to Newcastle that once. I thought it was so strange. The train station was massive. There were all these people going everywhere and all these big buildings. It was a bit daunting, because I'd never seen anything that size before. We just wandered round town. We were shopping. The shops and the size of the shops and the things they sold were amazing, though I remember thinking that they had a lot of stuff that was rubbish. I mean, what was the point of buying that plastic jewellery stuff. It was cheap but it was awful. I couldn't understand why people bought it. We went into Fenwicks. Oh, that was a lovely shop! The things they had! It was quite fascinating and I remember buying something there. I think I bought some tights and Barbara got herself a lacy bra. I'd never seen one like it. It was beautiful. I'd only ever had plain cotton ones. I'd never had anything with lace and things like that. I mean, the first bra my mother gave me was a cast-off from my nana. I was 12. It didn't even fit me. It had all these buttons down it and these great three-inch straps and I said, 'I'm not wearing that.' Oh, talk about a passion killer! It was horrible!

After we finished shopping, we went for a coffee. We went into a 'proper' coffee bar. They were playing Beatles music and we had an espresso. I think that was the first time I'd tried coffee. Then we got chatting to some boys. We wouldn't normally chat to boys unless they were our brothers or friends of our brothers, but, if I remember rightly, we knew these from the youth club. That was where you met boys, though I don't think any of us had special boyfriends at that time. At the youth clubs, everybody danced and talked with everybody else. There was no going off in corners and snogging. I was 17 or 18 before I got into that. Maybe I was a slow developer or something.

I don't think I really noticed fellas until I was working in Woolworth's when I was about 15. They used to come up and try to pick you up for a Saturday night, but I never felt I could go out with someone I'd met in Woolworth's. When I did start, my parents didn't mind me going out with a fella just once, but I think they got a bit worried after that. My mum didn't want us getting serious with anybody, and if we did go out twice, we had to bring the boy home to be met and given the third degree. My dad would sit there and say, 'Well, who are you? Who's your dad? Where does he work?' and all that kind of thing.

I was really green. My parents never told any of us anything about sex. When I had my first period I thought I was dying. I couldn't tell anybody. I just thought I was dying. I was bleeding and I didn't know why and there was nobody I could tell. I couldn't even tell my elder sister. You just didn't mention things like that in our house. I was quite embarrassed by it all. And I was terrified, but I'd seen these boxes of pads stuck in cupboards over the years and I just thought they would be practical to use, so I did. My mother must have noticed that pads were going missing, but she never said anything. I think my mother was probably the biggest prude of all time. I mean, you always got changed behind closed doors. Nobody ever never saw one another without being fully dressed in our house.

Then after about a year and half I decided I wanted to use tampons. I saw them advertised, so I went to my mum and said, 'Can't I use these instead of those horrible pads?' She just looked at me horrified and said, 'No.' That was all, that was the end of the conversation. So I just bought a box myself and tried them out in the bedroom. Oh God, I sweated buckets. They were horrible things to start with. I just looked at this diagram they gave you and I thought, 'I haven't got anything like that.' It took me a long time to figure out what to do.

I don't think the Pill had even reached our village by the mid-sixties. I'd never even heard of a condom. I'd heard names. I'd seen names on walls, but they didn't mean anything. I didn't know what they were. I used to hear of girls getting pregnant and the mums going 'tut, tut, tut', but I never knew how they got pregnant. I was 15 or 16 and I hadn't got a clue. I was having periods and so forth, but I still didn't twig as to why you needed them or how you got pregnant or anything. Really, it's amazing I ever coped with it all later on. Once there was something in *Woman's Own* about the facts of life and I said to my mum, 'Do you think I should give that to our Mary?' She was my younger sister. 'Put that away. She'll not be needing that,' was all she said. She had a very strange attitude, my mother. It was partly the way it was in those circles, though I don't think I knew anybody quite as bad as her.

One summer, when I must have been about 16 or 17, I went to stay with my friend in South Shields, and her mother – who used to be a nurse – must have twigged that I knew nothing. Well, she tried to tell me about the birds and the bees, but in a round-about way and it didn't really work. I just don't twig with stories. There was a film on television, *Birth of a Baby*, that we watched, but I still didn't twig. It had been shown in the cinemas and some people had thought it was outrageous, but all I could think of was that the woman in it looked rather tired. My mother would have been quite upset if she'd known I'd seen that film. I would never have been allowed to watch anything like that.

I must have been about 17 when I first started going around with boys, but it was always in a group. Some of the girls would pair off, but I used to think they were missing out on all the sort of gang activities which were quite fun. We would go to folk clubs. There was a folk club in the town every Friday night and it was something like two bob to get in. The entertainment was good. It was all these local folk singers. Sometimes you would get big acts from outside and then it would be two shillings extra. We used to travel all over the North-East. We'd go up to maybe Jarrow or South Shields. South Shields was a good place to go. They had a fairground and there was a good pub on the beach and things like that. I started trying out drinks about then. I'd have a couple of Cherry Bs and feel sick. In a pub if you were under age the fellas used to buy you an orange juice as well, and if we ever got the warning that there was going to be a police raid, the glasses just used to get switched around, so the girls would be sitting there with an orange juice and the fellas would have the Cherry B.

By the time I was 17, I was still babysitting and things to get money, but then I left school. I was never very academic. I didn't really enjoy school, but only because they didn't teach me anything that I was interested in. I wouldn't do my homework for love nor money, but I could have gone on to art college. I mean, I'd drawn for years and years and years. I used to enter the Kellogg's competitions and win paint palettes, and the Cadbury's competitions. You could win a box of Cadbury's chocolate. We went in for all of them. I did a lot of painting when I wasn't at the youth club. But my mother wasn't prepared to let me go on to art college. She said, 'You can't make any money out of drawing pictures.' In fact, she was against me going to any college. She thought it was something girls didn't do. College might have been all right if you wanted to be a teacher, but she wouldn't really have been keen for me to do that either. 'You're only going to go off and get married' is what she would have said. So that was that.

I don't think that if any of us had got a grant to go to college or university that my parents would have stopped us, but they would have seen it as three years of skiving or something. They just thought it was important to get to the grammar school, so you could get a good job in an office. My elder sister stayed on at school to get A-levels, but then she started work. She didn't go on to college. They just didn't think that kind of thing was important for women, because they would eventually get married and that would be it. I think if my brother had wanted to go to college, it would have been all right. I mean, even now in the North it's all right having daughters, but much nicer having a son. The son is always the heir. It's illogical, but my mother still thinks that way. When my parents die, everything will go to my brother. My mother's already given him something. She gave him my grandparents' stuff and he just went off and flogged it. He's a waster!

I did do a year in the sixth form, but it wasn't going to lead anywhere so I went out and got a job. I didn't really know what I wanted to do, and I never thought of moving away. I'd never really been anywhere, so I hadn't a clue. I got a job at Janet Frazer, the catalogue people. My parents were pleased because it wasn't in a factory. I'd got an office job, so as far as they were concerned I'd done well. But this job only lasted about four months. My mother then found out that I was earning nearly twice as much as my dad, because I also had my babysitting jobs and a Saturday job in a paper shop. I worked checking the orders, and the faster you were the more money you got. You had a basic number of orders that you had to check every day and then for every fifty extra that you checked you got extra money. I was 'Speedy Gonzales'. I could work very fast and I earned a lot of money. I used to get £13 a week when the basic was £3.12s. Then I used to get 7/6 a night babysitting on 3 nights and 10/- for working Saturday afternoon in the paper shop. My dad was only getting £8 a week – for a week down the pit!

I used to go straight into town with my money and buy clothes and shoes. I was mad on shoes. I still am. I must have about a hundred pairs of shoes. But anyway, I bought piles of stuff, half of which I never wore, and because I'd never had so many clothes before, my mother started to wonder where they were all coming from. Then she found out how much money I was earning and it all came to a head. My mother's one of the old school who think you should hand over your wage packet. She'd then give you what she thought was enough for spending money and the rest she would keep. Well, I was damned if I was going to hand over all this extra money I was getting, because it was a lot then and I'd worked hard to earn it. I could have easily just gone along to Janet Frazer, got my basic £3.12s a week, and let her give me whatever she thought I needed from that. I'd earned the extra by my own effort and I thought I deserved it.

My mum and I had a big row over that money, but then, probably like most teenagers, I was always rowing with her, from when I was about 15 onwards. She was very headstrong. All of us rowed with her, but it didn't get you anywhere in our house. You were just ignored. Eventually everybody left. We just all left home. It was the only way out. She'd have something to say about everything you did. For instance, she didn't want you to be out at night, even when you were over 18. I once went out with a fella, who was 28. Well, he had to be brought home, so that my dad could ask him who he was and where he was from and all the rest of it. He had a car and we went on to a folk club, and after the folk club he said, 'Do you want to go on to this night club?' So I said, 'Oh, all right.' I thought, 'Ooh, a night club, plush seats in there and cocktails.' But it was nothing special. It was all right, but nothing special. It was different, but it wasn't very exciting. We came out at about 2 o'clock in the morning, and we were moving out of the parking lot at the back of the club when the exhaust got caught against a rock. Well, the exhaust was half hanging off and we had to chug-chug home making a dreadful racket.

It was about 3 o'clock in the morning by the time we made it home. I said that I'd go in and find a bit of string to tie the exhaust up with, but when I got in the back door it was *wallop!*, a hand right across the back of my head. That was my dad waiting for me. I went running for the stairs, and when I got to the top there was another clout. It was my mum waiting in the pitch black. I tried to lean out of the bedroom window to get this guy's attention, to tell him there was no way I was going to be able to get him some string. I tried shouting to him, but I couldn't do it too loud in case I was heard, and he couldn't hear me. He must have sat there for about half-an-hour. Then he drove off. I never saw him again. I got the riot act the next day. I hadn't done anything. It was just that I had stayed out late and, as far as my parents were concerned, if you stayed out late you must have been doing things you shouldn't. That was what the clouts were for.

I was nearly 17, going on 18, and I just thought, 'I can't stand this any more. I've got to get out.' Then I saw an ad for nannies in America and answered it. I was sent down to an agency, where they told me all about it. I'd had a pen pal in America and I thought it sounded great, so they put the papers through and got me a job. It all went through very quickly, but because I wasn't 18 yet my parents had to sign these forms before I could go. They were furious. They refused to sign and we had an almighty row. But eventually they did sign the forms and off I went.

It was the longest trip I'd ever made. First I came down to London. I got the coach from Sunderland and was met by my sister, who took one look at me and said, 'You can't go to New York looking like that.' I didn't know what she meant. I thought I looked all right. I just had on the normal clothes that I always wore, which I thought were OK. But she didn't, and so all these girls that she shared a flat with were digging into their clothes and giving me skirts and tops and things. I ended up with a whole new wardrobe to take to New York.

I think I had £7 when I started out, but left that on the plane. I landed in New York with nothing. The flight was quite an experience. I'd never been on a plane, but I don't remember being frightened. It was Pan Am and they served this kebab thing with rice, and I thought, 'Oh God, what's that between the meat?' It was a skewer, but I'd never had a kebab before and I'd no idea what it was. Also, I'd only ever had rice in a pudding. I'd never had savoury rice. So I sat looking at this thing wondering how I was going to eat it. I mean, you couldn't get your knife and fork round a skewer. Then I looked at the girl next to me and I watched what she did. She was shoving the meat off the skewer and I thought, 'Oh, I'm not going to risk that. It could end up all over the place.' So I left the thing and I wouldn't try the rice. I was starving when I arrived in New York.

The chap I was going to work for met me at Kennedy Airport. I'd never seen him before, but he recognised me. He had my picture. Then he drove me home. I remember driving through Manhattan on the way out of town and seeing the skyline and thinking, 'My God! Just like the postcards.' We got to his house and sat down to dinner. I was starving, but I couldn't see how I was going to cope with what they brought out. There was some sort of chicken soup and I thought, 'Dear God, what's this?' It looked like dishwater to me. I'd only ever had broth. I'd never seen a clear soup before. I didn't know you could get clear soup. I thought, 'I can't eat that,' so I left it. Then they brought this chicken, which they were eating with their fingers. I was horrified. I thought, 'Ooh – cannibals!' I'd always been taught that you should never eat with your fingers. I couldn't eat the chicken either. Then they asked if I would like a piece of cheesecake. I nearly passed out. I'd never heard of such a thing. I thought it was a bit of cream on cheddar. I'd never seen anything like this meal. It was a total culture shock. I just wanted to go back home on the next plane.

Things didn't improve and I lost a lot of weight. I was thin to start with, but I got even thinner with these funny foods that they had. There was nothing normal. They didn't eat things like meat and two veg. I was there about two weeks when I decided it was all going to kill me and that I had to go home or something. I phoned up the agency and asked them if they had any other English girls near me – there was one, so we got together. I was curious to know how she was getting on. She was a good laugh. We used to go round town together. She was tall, blonde and leggy and would wear very short, tight knitted minis, so we always had fellas coming up to us. We must have got to know loads of people. She was only 18 and still green as well, despite the clothes. I remember when we'd been there about six weeks going down to Times Square. We'd heard all about it and wanted to look around, but two policemen came up to us and said, 'Where are you going?' We said we were just looking around and they said, 'This is not the sort of street you look at.' Well, we didn't know. Anyway, they escorted us back to the bus station.

We used to go out a lot. We'd go up to Greenwich Village and wander round there and go to the clubs. There were some smashing clubs in Greenwich Village. They were nice places to go to. You'd get folk singers or somebody playing a guitar. They weren't anything wild, although for me they were. But there was no sex or drugs or rock 'n' roll or any of that kind of thing. However, my friend ended up having an affair with the chap I worked for and his wife got suspicious. She thought it was me, so I got out. My employer booked me into a hotel for women in Manhattan. It was awful. It was full of drop-outs and decrepits, but on my first day there the desk clerk asked me out. It was the day that Robert Kennedy was killed. We went out for a couple of nights and he took me to a few bars – not singles' bars, but just regular bars like you see on TV. There was no sex involved, although one night he said, 'Can I come up to your room tonight?', so I gave him the wrong room number and when we got back to the hotel I said I wanted to go up first and would he mind waiting a few minutes. He probably came looking for me but he never found me. I was so naïve then. I always thought that if a fella took you out, all you had to do was be good company. I look back now and laugh at myself. I really never suspected fellas of being interested in anything else.

I had to go out and get another job. I had a green card from being a nanny, so I could change jobs just like that. You can't do that now. The laws changed while I was there. If you go over now as a nanny, you have to stay as a nanny. You've got to be there in a job for two years or something before you can move on. But then it was different and I was willing to try anything, so I just went out and signed on with the agencies. That was when I discovered that I couldn't really do anything. You go through grammar school, but you are really fit for nothing. You've got no real skills. Over there they don't care whether you've got history O-level. They don't know what it means. They want to know if you can type or do something. Well, of course, I couldn't, but they still managed to find me a job on that first morning. I went in as a trainee accounts clerk for a big mining company in Manhattan. They said they would train me. It was all very nice. They were quite affable.

Then I saw an advert in a New York paper, saying something about rooms for young professionals at this address. It was very cheap, something like $36 a week including all your meals, so I went along. It was a real dump of a house, but in a fabulous location just off Park Avenue, near Grand Central. I had to meet the other people who were there. The advert had said 'young professionals', but they still looked like a load of scruffs all stomping around in jeans and tee-shirts and the house itself was a bit seedy. But they seemed a reasonable bunch really and I got a room there. I think that was the turning point for me in America. It was smashing. Can you imagine being in a city like New York and there always being somebody you could go up to and say, 'Do you fancy going out tonight?' Or maybe somebody would come in and say, 'Have you heard about this?' and we'd all go out. There was always something happening.

Some of the women at the house were air hostesses and I think some of the fellas were teachers. I never knew what some of them did, but they were all working. The oldest was about 30. Quite a few of them were into flower power and all that. At least, on the surface they were. They all had these responsible jobs, so I can't see how they were really hippies. In fact, they weren't full-time hippies. They were weekend hippies. They'd go out during the day in their suits with their briefcases and then be out in their old fur coats and loons in the evenings and at weekends. It was more a fashion thing. In New York you worked hard. People were always doing something. A lot of the people I knew started their own businesses. Some of them were into strange projects, quite arty, and although I don't think anything came of most of them, at least they were doing something.

New York was a great place to be if you wanted to get on. Any firm you joined would do anything to help you. They were great. The second job I had was for a company that manufactured precious metals and I was talking to the boss one day about perhaps going to college. I just said I was thinking about it and he said, 'If you go, we'll pay.' So I then tried to get into college and of course O-levels don't mean anything to them. I was going to do economics and accounts, so I needed maths which I didn't have. But I produced my O-level certificates, which said on the top 'Oxford University', and they took one look at that and said, 'Oh yes, that's all right.' I was lucky. Otherwise I would have had to sit a maths exam which I never would have passed in a million years. Anyway, they let me in. This was at New York University. The company would keep your work going to whatever level you were at college, and when you passed an exam, you got a rise. Oh, it was wonderful. I was doing three evenings a week at New York University and I still managed to go out.

It was a great, great time. The social scene there was incredible, absolutely incredible. It was one big whirl. You never had time to sit and think about what you were doing. I didn't go to parties much, though. The circle I was in wasn't a party crowd. We went to concerts and things and the pictures. In the Park in summer a major beer company used to put on free concerts for about eight weeks. You could pay a dollar to get a seat in the enclosure or you could sit out in the valley on a cushion. We all used to take cushions. You'd get Judy Collins and Joni Mitchell there, all big names. Well-known people used to play in the Park. Then you would have classical concerts in a beautiful shell they had. I remember going two years running to just about anything that was on. And there'd be plays. There was just tons and tons of stuff – all free. And we'd go to Madison Square Garden. I saw Joan Baez there. I was well into Joan Baez. I saw her about three or four times when I was in America.

Weekends we went away. I'd sort of paired off with this fella from the boarding house. He was quite a bit older than me. I think he was about 28 or 29 and we went around in a circle that was all teachers, professors or artists, that sort of group. He was always taking me off to some place. He seemed to know people all over, so I got to some smashing places, places I never would have seen if I'd been on my own. We often went to Cape Cod, near where all the Kennedys were. A girl my boyfriend worked with – her father was a bishop – owned a house on the Cape, so we'd stay there quite a few weekends. There was this author, a white-haired man, who used to pop in sometimes for breakfast and I used to chat to him. I now realise he was Norman Mailer, but at the time I hadn't a clue who he was.

A lot of people at the Cape were into drugs. I'd not met many people like that in New York. When I did meet someone like that and they were all spaced out, I used to think, 'Oh God!' and ignore them. They'd be rambling and tripping and it just seemed so stupid to me. I never fancied any kind of drugs, not when I saw people like that. They just seemed to be making fools of themselves. I thought, why waste money on that kind of thing when you had to work so hard to get it? Perhaps if you were on the same level, you might not have thought like that, but to me these people who were into drugs all talked a lot of nonsense and they just looked silly.

I enjoyed the life. I'd never had that much freedom

before, never. It was wonderful. I loved it. I loved New York, because it was different and it was like the things I'd seen on television. I used to think it was all a bit like watching a film. And nothing scared me then. I mean, it didn't sink in that there was ever any danger. I never thought of any of the things I did as being unsafe. I would quite happily walk through the Park at any time. When I look back, I think there were probably a few people in New York who did laugh at me because I was so green, but generally people used to look after me. I suppose it was like protection. They never forced it on me, but if I wanted to go somewhere usually somebody would want to take me and then they'd make sure I got home and things like that. Also, I think luck was looking after me. I mean, you'd probably get killed if you went over there now and did the kind of things I did.

There were one or two scary moments. I always used to walk home when I'd been to college and I'd sometimes get blokes from there trying to walk with me and chat me up. Blokes would also shout at you from passing cars or out of windows. A couple of times I thought I could hear some-body coming up behind me. I would just wander on or give them a filthy look, thinking that would stop them. I shudder sometimes when I think of things like that. Then I moved out of the boarding house into a friend's flat in Greenwich Village and once when I was coming back from shopping, some old tramp was sort of following me. I just ran up to our door and tried to get in quickly but, in true form, I fell over. All my shopping was splattered across the street. Luckily, this couple who lived in our house had just arrived home and the bloke chased the tramp off, so I was all right.

After the tramp, I decided that perhaps the Village wasn't a very nice neighbourhood. Then somebody at work said he had a rent-controlled flat and asked would I like it. This new place was on East 73rd or something, which was a very nice location just one block from the river. So I went to have a look at it. The flat itself was big, but pretty grim. There was a fully kitted-out kitchen, a large lounge,

a bedroom and a bathroom, but it was riddled with cockroaches. I'd never seen cockroaches until then and I'd
been in New York nearly a year. The boarding house was
probably too run-down for them, and I'd seen none in the
Village. But here in 73rd, I lifted a draining board at the
side of the sink and it was crawling. I was horrified. After
I'd moved in, I just kept the lights on all the time so I
knew where they were. Eventually, my boyfriend got some
horrible powder and that took care of them.

I must have been about three or four months in that flat
when I decided to take my first trip home. I really came
back for Christmas. I hadn't enjoyed my first Christmas
away from home and I wanted to make sure I was back for
this one. My sister met me when I arrived in London. She
was still down there having a wild time. I can remember
her taking me shopping for some clothes. She was clothes-
mad and she persuaded me to buy a green leather mini-
coat. Talk about a bum-freezer! What a mistake!
However, I still wore it to go up to see my parents in
Sunderland. I don't know what they thought when they
saw me, but I think it was the wig that got them more than
the coat. I had this beautiful wig, which I'd got in New
York. But I don't think they were intimidated or over-
whelmed. I just got, 'Eeh, look at her!'

When Christmas was over, I went back down to London
with my sister. She was having a party for New Year and,
in fact, that's where I met Paul, my husband, for the first
time. My sister had just got engaged to Paul's cousin. I
can remember we talked all night, mainly about music,
and he asked me if I could get him a particular record in
New York. It was Bob Dylan's *Great White Wonder*. I
wrote the name down and said I would try. Paul had told
me this record was a 'bootleg' and I thought 'bootleg' was a
label like EMI, so I went to all the usual record stores
asking for it. The guys in the stores must have wondered
who the hell they were talking to. Some of them were very
rude and I didn't know why! Eventually I went into this
shop where an assistant pointed me down an aisle, so I
walked down there but I still couldn't see what I was

looking for. Then after a few minutes, he shouted out to me, 'Oh, I've got your purchase, madam.' I went back to the counter and he had the record ready, all wrapped up. 'That'll be $25,' he said. I nearly died. I was used to buying records for about $5 for two. I said, '$25! Are you sure?' and he said, 'Yes.' I thought it was ridiculous, but I'd promised it to Paul, so I took it. But before I sent it off, I thought, I've got to hear what you get for $25, and so I played it. What a load of rubbish it turned out to be. I couldn't believe it. I took it back, but the guy in the shop denied selling it to me. There was nothing I could do, so I sent it off to Paul for his 21st with a note saying I hoped he liked it and apologising for the quality. I said, 'It's terrible. I don't know what you see in him.'

It was soon after I got back from that trip home that I met Mohammed Ali. You used to see lots of film stars and people like that in New York. I saw some really big names when I was there – Dustin Hoffman, Paul Newman, George Segal, Lee Remick, Elliot Gould. I actually spoke to Elliot Gould and he was very nice, very funny, but meeting Mohammed Ali was the biggest thrill of the lot. My boyfriend and I had been to see a show at Radio City Hall and we were on our way out when we came across this crowd. Being short, I couldn't see anything except people's shoulders, so I kept saying, 'Excuse me, please, excuse me, please,' and eventually there I was at the front of the queue and I looked up and there was this huge man. It was him. He was gorgeous, strikingly handsome. I was quite embarrassed. I tried to get back into the crowd, but I couldn't. He had a couple of bodyguards with him and was shouting and playing to the crowd. He'd just come out of prison for refusing to go to Vietnam. I just stood there thinking 'Oo-er ...' and started fishing around in my handbag to get some paper for an autograph. Then he looked down and spoke to me. He asked me where I was from and when I said England, he stopped performing for the crowd and we just got talking. He starting asking what I was doing in New York and how long I'd been there. He said that he loved the English, that they'd always made him feel welcome. We just chatted. He was so nice and I'd never seen anyone so good-looking in my entire life. Then he said, 'Are you wanting to go back out this way?' And I said, 'Yes, yes – all right.' So he said, 'Well, come on,' and he took me out through the crowd, just his bodyguards and me! Then he offered me a lift home, but I said, 'No, thank you,' and told him I was with someone. I've often wondered what would have happened if I had said yes.

I always thought it was very brave of Mohammed Ali refusing to go out to Vietnam. Vietnam was the only political thing I got involved in while I was in America. Basically, I don't believe in war as a means of solution. I think it's futile and I'd met people who had been out in Vietnam. They hadn't wanted to go and they'd come back with these awful stories about the killings and everything. So many people were killed or horribly maimed. I knew somebody who worked in a hospital and he used to say it was horrendous the state some of the veterans were in and the way they were treated when they got back. It was an unpopular war. The Americans themselves didn't want it and there was a march organised, some time in early 1969, I think, about the time that they were increasing the bombing on Vietnam. It was very well publicised and I just went along with thousands and thousands of others. It was very peaceful and well controlled and got oodles and oodles of press and television coverage.

I got a really unexpected reaction from people at work for going on that march. As far as I was concerned, I had just gone to put in my protest and that was it, but when I walked into the office on the Monday and they asked me the usual about what I had done over the weekend and I said, 'Oh, I went on the march,' there was murder on. They were all telling me to go back home to where I belonged, and that it was their country and I should mind my own business. They weren't necessarily pro-Vietnam, but they were American and supported the flag. Americans are a strange breed. They come out on the side of freedom for all, yet they are probably the most bigoted people on God's earth. They are staunch flag supporters.

They can condemn their flag, but nobody else can. They were very angry that I had been on that march. So there was a bit of unpleasantness for a couple of days, but it all blew over. They had said their piece.

I never got involved in anything else political apart from that march. I wasn't very interested in politics generally. Most of the time, I was just going out or studying, though I can't remember study ever featuring strongly. I think about half way through the course I realised I didn't really like accountancy, but it was too late to change. I also did quite a bit of travelling in the States. The travel was one of the nicest things about America. It was also very cheap. You could hop on a Greyhound bus or on any coach and just go. One of my best trips was to California. I'd been in America nearly two years when I went and I'd seen lots of the east coast, which was beautiful, but I kept hearing about California. Also, my boyfriend came from there and he was always going on about it, so I just thought I had to go.

Off I went on this three-week trip. I went by coach. I didn't want to fly because I would miss the rest of the country. The first coach broke down and we got a second one, which also broke down. Then they brought us a third coach, and we were crossing Oklahoma when it caught fire! Some of the people got hysterical. They kept saying that we should stop talking because we were using all the air in the coach. I mean – it was ridiculous – the window was open! I can remember there was a lightning storm going on outside, which was fantastic to watch. It was just like the movies. I was loving it. I mean, there was never any real danger. It was only the engine that had caught fire, and by now that had got dowsed by the rain. Because Oklahoma is flat, you could see for miles and miles. There were these little wee farmhouses in the distance, and it looked great with forks of lightning coming and bouncing off the ground. Oh, it was marvellous. I'd only ever seen anything like that before at the pictures. To actually be there was wonderful. But nothing really happened. We just waited for a couple of hours until the Highway Patrol came. Of course, it wasn't Broderick Crawford, but I had my photo taken with the man that came. They took us all to Howard Johnson's, which is a motel chain and coffee shop, and gave us free pancakes and syrup and coffee. Then we just waited around there for the next coach.

When I finally got there, I first stayed with my boyfriend's mother. She had a lovely flat somewhere in LA, a beautiful little Spanish-style place. My boyfriend's brother also lived in California. He took me out a couple of times in his Mustang. Oh, he was the most boring individual I've ever met in my life. He had nothing to say and moaned the whole time. He bored the pants off me – or rather, he didn't bore the pants off me. Well, I couldn't stand that for long, so I started going out with these other guys that I'd met on the coach. Then my boyfriend passed the word to an old friend of his that I was in town, and asked him if he would come and show me around. So one day I opened the door and there was a black fella standing there in a a pair of shorts, big boots and a crash helmet. He just stood there and said, 'My name is Cy and I'm here to take you out.' 'Oh yeah,' I said, 'in what?' And he said, 'My bike.' He had this massive thing, a Harley Davidson or BMW or something like that, and I said, 'I'm not getting on that. You'd better go and find a car.' So he said, 'I've only got the bike.' 'Well,' I said, 'I can't ride a bike. I've got no sense of balance at all. I'm not going on that thing.' Anyway, that was that and eventually he got somebody with a car to pick me up and take me to his house. He was living in a commune somewhere in LA.

That commune was fascinating. I'd never been anywhere like it. It was a nice big house, a proper house, and they were very well organised. Everyone had a role. Even if you were visiting, you had a job to do. I stayed there for three days and my job mainly involved cooking or washing up. They weren't drop-outs. They were nearly all semi-professional or professional people, and I think some of them were running small businesses or something. It was really all part of a sort of proper hippy movement. They were trying to make money to exist without working in the usual way. One of the things they were making was tie-dye stuff, because tie-dye was in vogue then. I did some tie-dying while I was there. I slept in the garage and I wore my jeans and normal tops. There were no flowers or beads or flowing robes, not even flowered jeans, and there were no drugs or transcendental experiences either. But it was great. I enjoyed the time I spent there. The bloke who took me was smashing and I did eventually get on his bike. In fact, most of the time we were just driving around, because in the end I loved it.

When I'd arrived at the commune, he'd made it clear that if he was going to show me around, I'd have to get on the bike. So we'd started off on this trainer, this little bike, and were going round the block at ten miles an hour to try and give me some confidence. Gradually, I'd got the hang of it and began to think it was great. I hadn't wanted to get off. Then I'd got on to the bigger bike and soon there we were, doing a hundred and odd miles down the freeway. Oh, I couldn't get enough of it. It was the thrill of a life-time. I loved it. I could have biked it every minute of the day. I even started wanting my own bike, though I'm not sure I'd have been capable of controlling a bike on my own, let alone have the guts to drive one. But this chap knew what he was doing. He loved his bike. In those days there wasn't any speed limit on the freeway, and you didn't have to wear a crash helmet either. There was a lot of wind on the freeway and I had long straight hair then – you know, Joan Baez hair – which used to flow out behind me as we went along. Oh, it was highly dangerous, but I just loved it. All I used to wear was my swimsuit under-neath my jeans and that was it. I didn't want to ever get off that bike.

Occasionally I got some funny looks, travelling around with a black guy, and I was spat at once, but that was all. There was no real trouble. California was fairly free and easy then, I think. I was never very aware of things to do with race, though I was told that there had been some riots a couple of years previously, when the blacks had rebelled and demanded things like better housing and better conditions, just like everybody else. I think California was trying to accommodate all of this when I was there, but I doubt if underneath they were really overcoming their prejudice. White Americans are generally fairly prejudiced, to be quite honest. Even now they still keep the blacks very much down. They pay lip-service to their demands, but I don't think they've ever really given them the same rights as everybody else. I don't think they ever will. America is really just for successful white Americans, because they don't like the poor whites either. But on the face of things, most people were fine with us. There was only really this one spitting incident and I think I was more embarrassed for the fella than for me. We just brushed it off as one of those things.

Then some friends of mine arrived from New York and this guy they'd known from college took us all off to Disneyland in his car. I'd never seen a car like it. It was a banger, but like no banger I'd ever seen. I was surprised it even went. When you turned a corner all the doors swung open. Then they'd swing back again. I was sitting in the front and the springs had gone from the seat. It was like sitting on the floor. I tried to roll the windows down, because there was no air-conditioning, and they just went plop and disappeared into the door. Well, the first few times the doors swung open or the windows went plop, I kept a straight face and carried on the conversation we were having as though nothing had happened. Then one of my friends in the back started to giggle and that was it. Suddenly, it was absolute hysterics. We couldn't stop laughing and the driver started getting quite upset. He couldn't see what we were laughing at. I was uncontrollable. My two friends in the back were helpless. They were sort of falling all over each other. By the time we swung into Disneyland and reached the parking lot, I was hiding my face in the dashboard. The poor driver was furious with us.

Disneyland was incredible. It was wonderful. You go round and you feel sort of 5 years old again. It's very, very clever, very well done. Then we went on to Knott's Berry

Farm, which was a big tourist attraction at the time. You could buy fruit and jam there or have waffles with the jam or berries. And we went to San Diego to see the dolphins. We did all the tourist things, but we didn't go to San Francisco. I just didn't fancy it. It was the height of the hippy era then and to me all they seemed to be doing there was loafing around. They had this 'guru' at the time, Timothy Leary. You used to see him interviewed on television. I didn't go a lot on his style. I'd seen a few people get screwed up on drugs and a girl I knew in New York had had a boyfriend who'd drowned in the bath after taking LSD. As I said earlier, I just thought the whole drug thing was stupid and it was expensive. LSD was the 'fashion' drug at the time.

Then I came back to New York. My boss couldn't believe that I'd gone out with $100 for three weeks' stay, come back with $97, and that I'd been everywhere! Then soon after that there was Woodstock. Joan Baez was billed as being on, so I had to go. It was quite easy to get a ticket. I just went along to this place where they were selling them and that was that. You could get tickets for things quite easily in those days. There was never any panic or anything.

It started on a Friday. But I was working, and as I was in a new job which I'd only had for about a week, I didn't think I could take days off, so I was going up on the Friday night. Woodstock's in upstate New York, near Buffalo way. My boyfriend had gone up on Friday morning and just as I was at home packing, I got a call from him telling me to bring up some food and drink. He said, 'There's nothing here and there's thousands arrived. They've gatecrashed. There's no tickets. There's no point in bringing a ticket. There's thousands and thousands here and nothing to eat or drink. You've seen nothing like it.' You see it all happened in this field, just a farmer's field with a big platform for a stage. That's all it was, and with so many freeloaders it was pandemonium. There were supposed to be 20,000 people there and 20,000 in that valley would have been all right – instead of the almost half a million that were there.

Anyway, I got a big box of chicken and stuff ready and went down to the coach, but they said, 'We can't get you to Woodstock. We can only get you within 14 miles.' That started me thinking that I ought to forget about it and just stay at home. I mean, I'd got this great damn box of stuff that I could barely carry, and now I was being told that I'd have to cart it 14 miles. But I did get on the coach and we got as far as they could take us. The rest of the road was blocked with people and cars. I've got no sense of direction, but you couldn't get lost. It was obvious where to go. You just followed everybody else. At first, I hitched with this sports car, but we only got about 100 yards before we had to stop. Then another car came by, so I plonked my box of stuff on the back of that car and got a bit farther up the road. Then he had to stop as well. We hadn't gone more than half a mile. Everyone just had to pull in in their cars. The parking lot was 14 miles long! Cars were parked all the way down from Woodstock, right down the road for 14 miles on both sides of the road.

The two lads whose car I had been in then offered to carry my box, so I gave them some of the chicken and something to drink. They were very nice, those lads. They carried my box the rest of the way. They kept having more chicken and drinks and the box was getting lighter and lighter. But it was a hell of a walk and I kept thinking, 'How the hell am I going to meet him?' Then eventually I saw my boyfriend walking down, obviously coming to look for me. It was pure luck that we found each other among all that lot. He just said, 'There's nothing up there. There's no food, there's no drink. There's nothing. And the crowds – you should see the crowds. You won't believe it.' By now I only had two bits of chicken and two cans of Coke left. My boyfriend was spitting blood. He was furious. I'd started off this big box all full. It had all gone on the way. So we just finished what there was and walked on.

There were people everywhere – starkers in the pools – everywhere. There was mud everywhere. You got up to the site and looked over the field and there was this huge valley, very deep and grey. The whole thing was grey with all these bodies going across this huge expanse of land, and in the middle was a tiny platform that was the stage. My boyfriend told me somebody had been killed farther up the valley. They had been in a cornfield or something and got chopped to death by the harvester. The farmer was trying to do his work and they shouldn't have been there. He hadn't noticed them.

There were police everywhere. I think I remember they were wearing red jackets, so it was easy to pick them out in the crowds. Their main job was just to keep people calm. They were sort of turning a blind eye to drugs as long as they were inside the field. If you were caught with them outside, you could be searched and arrested. There was stuff being passed around all the time – smokes going backwards and forwards and all that. Half the crowd were stoned up to the hilt. You could just about see the stage, but it was more interesting watching the crowd.

I'd come to see Joan Baez and there I was in a muddy field in the middle of nowhere. The toilets were blocked. There was no food. There was no drink. Ooh, it was horrible! They did bring in some more portaloos, but if you went to the loo, someone would have to use signals, wave a flag or a flashlight or something, so you could find your place again. We were concerned about whether it was going to rain, because we would be swamped out if it rained once more. Oh, it was most uncomfortable. It wasn't my idea of heaven. We stayed there two days, I think. We had nothing to eat and just slept on the sleeping bag on the ground. We could have put the seats down in the car, but it was a case of if you left the field you wouldn't get your place back, which meant you wouldn't have seen anything at all. I mean, the stage was minute from where we were, so I can't imagine what it must have been like farther back.

I remember waking up to The Who doing *My Generation* or something. And then there was Hendrix and that sort of thing. I'd only come because of Joan, and I wasn't

57

really that keen on most of it. It just wasn't quite my sort of music. And with the mess, all the mud and no toilets and no drinks and no food, it was pretty grim – and I'd actually paid my money. I'd paid my ten or fourteen dollars or whatever. I've still got the ticket somewhere. Also, it took ages to get out of there, ages with the car being parked right in. There were people looking for their cars everywhere. You had thousands of bodies, again all down the road, as we were coming out, all looking for their stuff. There must have been a hell of a mess left behind. I think the people of the town asked for volunteers to stay behind and help clear up, and some of the hippies, the genuine ones, did.

The publicity people certainly did a good job of glamorising the whole event afterwards. They made it out to be much more than it ever was. I think the organisers actually lost a lot of money, because so many of the people there hadn't bought tickets. To save having a riot, they'd let them in for free, so perhaps the film and the glamour was to make up for what they didn't get on the gate. I suppose the venue was OK really and the sound was OK. It was just all those extra people. After that, I swore I'd never go to another open-air concert as long as I lived and I never have. I wouldn't even entertain the idea. It was an experience, but it wasn't one I'd like to repeat.

I wasn't long in America after that. I came back in early 1970. But first I went back to New York and just carried on. They were going to pull down the flat I was living in on 73rd, so we all got notice to look for somewhere else. I think it was $200 we all got offered to move out, but I knew already I was leaving America, so it didn't brother me and I ended up receiving $1,000 to vacate my flat. I was coming home for my sister's wedding and for Paul. He'd never written to me as promised or sent me any of the records he said he would, but we'd sort of communicated through my sister. When I got back to Heathrow, there he was to meet me. He was best man at the wedding and I was bridesmaid, and we got engaged the day after.

I didn't miss America. I was glad to be home. But the

experience had been wonderful. While it was all happening it was really wonderful. I had so much freedom. I wouldn't like to be young now. I don't think you could have that sort of freedom now. I feel sorry for young people. They've got a lot more street sense – ten times more than I had or ever will have – but they've not got that freedom. I mean, you can't let some 18-year-old go off now the way I did, travelling and just wandering around a city like New York. It just wouldn't be safe – and anyway, most young people today probably couldn't afford to do that kind of thing. Then, you could always just leave a job and go and do something else. There would always be another job. If you wanted to go off for three weeks, you could just do it. You wouldn't get paid for that three weeks, but that wasn't going to make a huge difference to you. Living was cheap. Travelling was cheap. There were lots of different ways to travel cheaply, in America especially. You could get all over the place. You can't do that now. The sixties were fun times.

LEE

The beginning of the sixties means nothing to me, except being a little girl. I was born in 1950, so I was mostly 9 and then I was 10. I think the sixties really started for me in 1963. Two major things happened that year. The really big event that everybody remembers occurred late on in the year, in November. I remember being at school. I was in the eighth grade then, and we were all sent back to our classrooms, where they announced that President Kennedy had been shot and we were to go home. Miraculously – which was what it seemed like then – all the parents must have known about this too, because suddenly they were all parked in front of the school, even though it was only about noon. I was supposed to have a friend from school come over to play that afternoon. Well, she came with us and we went downstairs and we were fooling about in the basement on the piano. Then my mother came downstairs and said, 'Well, I think I should take Janey home now, because the President has just died.'

We didn't go to school again for days after that. We just watched the television to see what was going on. My father even kept all the newspapers from the time – it was considered to be *that* important a thing, although somehow I didn't really connect it with being of national or personal importance. I just thought that other presidents had been killed – from what we'd learnt in school one seemed to get assassinated about every twenty years or so – and I was sufficiently young that I didn't really take in anything to do with politics or government or the future of the world. I was only interested in myself and my environment and I couldn't see how this was going to affect anything at all, except that everybody seemed to be really very shocked and very sad.

What probably affected me more happened earlier in the year. That was when The Beatles came to the States,

which really was exciting. I already knew about The
Beatles, because I had a pen pal in Manchester, England.
She was slightly older than me, and absolutely dead keen
on the whole Liverpool sound. She only wrote me about six
letters, but there was such a lot about The Beatles in
them. Then my mother came home one day with this LP
called *Meet The Beatles*. She told me that everybody in
the record store was buying it and that she had been told
that it was for teenagers, so she thought I might like one
too. Now before that, the only records I'd ever had were
the soundtrack to *West Side Story* and, I think, the theme-
song to *Exodus*, so I didn't know anything about pop
music. I'd been too young for Elvis or for all the really,
really boring sort of soft balladeers in the early sixties.
They had completely passed me by, but I really liked The
Beatles. I can remember them being on television and
listening to them on the radio, giving these wacky interviews in this very strange accent. Everybody at school was
talking about them. I think they were my real introduction
to what the sixties were all about.

The Beatles, and later The Stones, were what got me
into rock 'n' roll. In fact, I liked The Stones more, because
they had that somewhat rakish, more rebellious, aspect.
But I never had pictures of pop stars on my wall. I wasn't
that kind of fan. The minute I saw a rock 'n' roll band, the
main thing on my mind was that I wanted to be in one. I
had no idea how I would go about it. I didn't know it was
possible because there didn't seem to be any girls in rock
then, but I thought this was definitely for me. Remember,
this was still a couple of years before Cher came along with
Sonny. There were really only the more traditional Connie
Francis, Brenda Lee-type ballad singers with their bouffant hair-dos. I don't remember Lulu or any of the British
girl singers crossing the Atlantic, so I didn't have any real
female role model. It was 1966 before we got Grace Slick –
she was really the first – and it was about 1967 or 1968
before Janis Joplin. Anyway, I never liked Janis Joplin. I
thought she looked a tatty mess.

My parents were incredibly indulgent with my interest

in rock music. All during the sixties, my mother would actually get tickets for all the major concerts. I never got to see The Beatles, but I saw The Stones every time they came and I saw The Dave Clark Five, Gerry and the Pacemakers, The Animals and The Moody Blues – practically everybody who came, in fact. My mother would somehow trot out and get these front-row tickets and she and my father would drive me and my little friends in our school dresses to Boston Garden to go to these concerts. I'd sit there, surrounded by all these girls who would be going absolutely bananas, and I'd be very controlled, simply wanting to be up there on that stage. Then my parents would pick us up afterwards out front and drive us home, everyone having had a wonderful evening. I still to this day don't know what they did with the three hours that we were inside, but it was most remarkable that I was indulged in this way.

When I was 14 or 15 – this would have been in about 1965 – I finally decided I couldn't stand it any more. At that time, they started having keyboards in bands, while before it had only been the usual three guitar and drums scenario. I'd taken piano lessons, so I knew that if I was going to convince my father that I was going to be a rock 'n' roll star, it had to be through keyboards, because he already knew that I could play them. Anyway, he made me sit down and write a list of reasons why I should have this very expensive equipment. Then, after a lot of umming and aahing and more umming and aahing, we finally went into a music shop in Boston and bought a second-hand Farfisa organ and a Fender amplifier. That meant I now had the best equipment in town and, although I wasn't in a band at this point, suddenly everybody wanted me – (a) because I had the equipment, when most of them only had really grotty stuff, and (b) because I was a girl, which meant I had novelty value.

Strangely enough, I had no real idea how to play any of this equipment my father had bought, because I was classically trained. I knew nothing about chording, but I just thought I'd sit and wait for the phone to ring and it did!

Four different bands in town rang me up and said, 'Do you want to be in our group?' I went with the one that had all the gigs, which was a group called The Rebels. All of which distanced me from quite a few of my school friends. Maybe they were jealous or maybe it was because I was sort of breaking the rules and taking on a non-traditional female role. Most of my friends just wanted to worship pop stars from afar. Generally it was The Beatles. Girls would sit in class and write 'Paul, Paul, Paul' a thousand times in an exercise book, and every article of their clothing or their school satchels would have 'I love John' or 'I love Ringo' across it. I wasn't into any of that. I suppose I wanted to be the famous one. I thought I had something special – but then, plenty of teenagers feel like that.

The Rebels were not a particularly good group, but we did have a very definite, strong group image. We wore a kind of uniform. I used to wear a white mini-skirt and sweater and, as soon as they were available, I had white Courrèges boots. My hair was bleached very, very blonde and was in a sort of sixties flip style. I used to wear rollers to sleep every night so my hair would be perfect for school. All the girls I knew used to spend an inordinate amount of time on their hair. I've just seen *Hairspray*, the Jon Waters film about hair hoppers, and although we didn't have the bouffant hair-dos of the early sixties, there wasn't a single girl in my school who didn't wash her hair nearly every night and then get into bed with these huge two- or three-inch diameter rollers all over her head. Getting ready for school the next day could take up the entire evening.

Image meant a lot to me, so my clothes were very important. I had to have the right kind of clothes for school. Now this was a school in a very rich community and, if you wore the same outfit more than once every three weeks, you were considered to be not of the right social group. It showed that you didn't have money. Among the very rich girls, whose parents had accounts at the best stores, there was a tremendous amount of shoplifting. My parents didn't have accounts at any of these stores and I never shoplifted, but I used to go into them with girls who would take half a dozen Fair Isle sweaters into a changing room and come back with four, nicking two. The stores knew exactly what was going on, but they didn't say anything because the parents spent so much money there. They were probably just adding the cost of shoplifted items on to the end of the parents' monthly bills.

But it was very important to have the right kind of clothes – the right shoes and the right skirts and sweaters. In the very early sixties, up until the Mary Quant thing, you had to have a nice tweedy skirt and a Fair Isle sweater with a little circle pin at the neck on a rounded white collar. Then once 'the English look' came in, people started changing their clothes and hairstyles, wearing mini-skirts and getting geometric haircuts. We used to go into a place in Boston called Filene's Basement, which was a mark-down shop for a major store. You could go in there and you could get Mary Quant clothes really, really cheap, and beautiful snakeskin shoes – all sorts of wonderful things. We used to go in every Saturday and spent whatever money we had, which wasn't much, but you used to be able to get some amazing stuff.

The type of make-up that I wore then was completely different to anything I would wear now. I usually wore full pancake make-up on my face in a fake tan, so that even in the winter I had these very brown cheeks. I used to do my neck as well and underneath my hair at the back, which meant, of course, that I would always have this brown ring around the inside edge of my collar because of this make-up rubbing off. I also wore tons of eye make-up – lots and lots of mascara and very pronounced black liner around my eyes. But I never remember wearing lipstick. I could never keep it on because I was always biting my lips. I was always changing my hair colour too. It used to take me forty-five minutes in the morning just to get ready to go out – and remember I did this nearly every morning, because I used to go to school made-up like this wearing one of my mini-skirts. But that wasn't a problem. No one objected, although I'm not talking about weekend mini-skirts, which were probably only a couple of inches down from the bottom, but school mini-skirts that were about four inches up from the knee. All you had to do was to avoid the school matron. If the matron didn't see you, you were all right. The teachers didn't care.

We didn't wear a uniform, because I went to what you call in the States a public school, which means that every-body goes to it. In a way, a uniform would have been much better because there was a division of wealth in the school. I mean, some kids came from homes with swimming pools and chauffeurs and other kids had nothing. So looking right, having the right kind of image, could be a tremen-dous problem for the kids who didn't have the money. My mother was an excellent seamstress. She bought my swea-ters but made all my skirts, so I always had the right little outfits. She wanted me well dressed, and she never objected to me wearing mini-skirts. At one point in the late sixties, I can remember her making me a fake snakeskin mini-skirt that was so short my knickers showed. The only thing she ever said to me about the way I was dressed was once when I went out wearing a see-through blouse with-out a bra underneath, and she said to me, 'I do wish you would stick plasters over your nipples because if it's cold they'll show.' And I said, 'Oh Mother, you're so old-fashioned.' And she said, 'Well, suit yourself.' But she never actually said, 'You're not going out like that!' I never had any of that kind of criticism at all.

One of the things that my mother did consider tarty were pierced ears. Like ankle bracelets, they were just something you didn't have if you were the right kind of person. I once pointed out to my mother that the Queen of England had pierced ears and she said, 'That can't possi-bly be true. The Queen of England would never have pierced ears. She wouldn't do something like that.' But anyway, they were starting to become very fashionable at the time and I was quite keen to have them. I got really agitated about it and eventually my father said to me, 'OK, you can have pierced ears if you pierce them yourself.'

So I got a gold stickpin, which my father had – it was a diamond stickpin – and I put rubbing alcohol on both sides of my ear and I rammed it through. But after I'd done the one ear, I thought, that's it. It really took a lot of nerve and I couldn't face doing the same to the other one. I'd only done it to prove a point. So for a long time, long before it was fashionable to do so, I just wore the one earring, which my father used to think was a great hoot. Every Christmas and birthday, he would go to a jeweller and have one earring made up for me as a present. In fact, what I didn't know at the time was that he was actually having pairs made up but giving me only one of them. When I finally pierced the other ear, which I also did myself in the late sixties, he all of a sudden presented me with this whole pile of earrings matching the ones I already had. Later, I regretted piercing my other ear. It looked wonderfully rakish just having the one pierced ear, and it fitted in with my rock 'n' roll image.

Despite all this grooming and preening, I did find time to play in the band. In fact, we had rehearsals most nights after school and on Friday and Saturday nights we always had a gig. We had a female manager called Melinda. Her marriage was breaking up at the time and I think she needed something to get her out of herself. She'd heard the band, liked it, and, probably thinking that she might try to get into public relations or something, had thought managing us was a good test. She would cold-call and book the venues. Thanks to her, we got into places we never should have got into, because, frankly, we were lousy. None of us were particularly good musicians and we were a bit old-fashioned. They used to call us 'the 55s', which meant our music was more like 1955 than 1965. It was a bit humiliating. Occasionally, we would try to get things a little more modern, like learning songs by the Yardbirds and other groups, but it never seemed to make much difference. There were much more forward-looking bands around, some of them pretty decent. I think we got the gigs partly because I was in the group. As I've said, it was unusual to have a girl and I was cute – and the boys were cute as well.

We were only about 15 or 16.

My parents were really good about the band and my going into clubs and places like that. They knew that Melinda was always with us and that she was pretty strict, so we were unlikely to get up to anything we shouldn't. The band only became a problem later, when it started to take up so much of my time that my school performance went off drastically. But I was always in the top stream. In the States when you're about 9 years old, you're given a battery of tests and, if you do extremely well, you go into a separate group at school. I was one of that elite. Nobody was ever added to our group, but people used to disappear every year if they couldn't keep up. All of a sudden, they just weren't in your classes any more and you didn't think anything of it. You'd go back to school in the autumn and, you know, Joe Bloggs would be gone and you'd just think, 'Oh well, he didn't make the grade, ha, ha!' We were terribly snide and cocky. We had these weird teachers, who one minute would tell us we were the elect of the gods and the next minute would tell us we were lazy so-and-so's who did nothing. I did nothing, and thank goodness I didn't really have to. Even when my performance dropped off because I was so busy with the band, I managed for the most part to keep a decent average. I soon dropped the subjects that required lots of work, like French and sciences. And I still got into a good university at the end of the day – Boston University. So, although it wasn't the nice girls' college that my mother wanted me to go to – like Wellesley or Radcliffe – I none the less didn't embarrass anyone by where I went.

I also think that being in a mixed school had an effect on my academic performance. If you're a girl in a mixed school, there comes a time when your concentration goes out the window. This happened to me when I was about 14 or 15. I started to get serious crushes on boys and they became the primary consideration. I'd spend hours being extremely moody. Now I realise a lot of that was down to hormones, the changes taking place in my body. This was about the time that I was really developing. I was starting to get breasts and I'd just got my periods. Previous to that point, I hadn't really noticed boys, except as some more or less alien species that were pretty dirty and nasty. So, in a way, it was a loss of innocence and the start of my teenage years that had a major effect on my school work.

I sometimes got the impression that my parents thought I was being deliberately difficult. I think my father once called me 'Sarah Heartburn' instead of Sarah Bernhardt, because he claimed I was such an actress. But I did feel things really, really strongly. If I got a crush on a boy and he rejected me, it was terrible, completely terrible. At the time, if a guy asked you out, took you to a dance or wherever, it was the be all and end all. Joining the band, in fact, sorted all that out. Once I joined them, lots of boys asked me out, although I couldn't go on dates then because we were playing both Friday and Saturday nights. Also, I started to feel good about myself, because the money we were making was phenomenal. From the two nights' work, I was probably taking home an average father's wage for a week! Melinda was a very hard bargainer and she always got us extremely good money. I think my father and mother were secretly and sneakily quite pleased that I was doing so well. They made me bank all the money, and they actually forced me to go on a holiday to Florida when I was about 16 – probably to get me out of the house because I was being such a pain. I went to stay with a great-aunt and uncle in a geriatric trailer park, but I had a great time. I went entirely on my own – got on the flight and was met at the other end.

I was allowed a huge amount of freedom in certain ways, but was terribly restricted in other ways. Sex, of course, was never mentioned at home. When I had been very much younger, I belonged to a Girl Scout troupe, and the Girl Scouts had a Disney film which was about menstruation and showed little Bambi-like characters and butterflies and a cartoon uterus. It was absolutely ghastly, but we all sat there and watched it and they handed out leaflets afterwards. My mother knew we were going to be shown this and when I got home she asked me if I knew what was going on and did I understand it all. I went, 'Yeah, yeah, yeah,' but this was when I was about 11, before I actually started menstruating, and I'd completely missed the point. I can remember my mother finally realising that I didn't know anything when one day my father was out mowing the lawn and he left it a bit too late to come in to the loo. He ran into the house, made a dash for the loo, and didn't have time to close the door. You could hear him having this huge long pee and then this sigh of relief. And I said to him when he came out, 'You should wear Kotex like Mummy does,' and he looked at me and said, 'This child hasn't got a clue.' I'd seen these Kotex sanitary towels in the cupboard underneath the bathroom sink and I kind of thought that as they were big and bulky like diapers, they were something like incontinence pads.

It was a bit later before I realised what sanitary towels were for. When we did PE at school, you had to line up at the beginning of the class and they'd yell your name. If you had your period, you said 'regular'. Don't ask me why they used the word 'regular', but it meant you didn't have to take a shower. Tampax wasn't universally used by young girls then, and I quickly realised that this routine was to save you the embarrassment of wearing sanitary towels. Most girls then used these bulky sanitary towels held in place with a special belt. They didn't have the stick-on pads then. I cottoned on to all this before I had my periods, and used to say 'regular' every four weeks just so I could duck out of the showers. Then when I did get my period, I immediately insisted on using Tampax. I knew about them because they were advertised in the teenage magazines. I never used pads. I decided I wasn't going to waddle around with this great wad between my legs, and thought it was much nicer to have these little things you inserted. My mother said, 'You may find it difficult. I've never been able to use them,' but she was quite OK about me using them. I was really very definite about it, and I think as I was an only child and both my parents were a bit older than my contemporaries' parents, they were really afraid to buck me too much if I was definite about something. More often than not, if it wasn't something of earthshaking importance, I got my own way.

Sex, however, as far as what you did and what you didn't do, was something we never really talked about. I found out how people made love by reading a book I bought at a jumble sale. It was a school fête really, and there was this whole table of books and one of them was a book called *The Group*, by Mary McCarthy, I think. I believe sex was mentioned in that book but in a very oblique way – something about iron-hard rods – and I couldn't quite figure out what a man and woman were doing in bed with an iron-hard rod. But by the time I got to the end of the book, I had more or less figured it out. I thought it was most amazing. I told my friend Julie and she and I decided that we ought to get this book – *What Every Teenager Should Know About Sex* – or something like that.

So we went and bought this book and took it to a field one afternoon and sat and read it from cover to cover. It was all 'Did you?', 'No!', 'Really!' We vowed to our dying day we would never get involved in that stuff. We thought it was quite disgusting – but, on the other hand, it was also quite intriguing. And we figured that a lot of people – including people we knew – must be doing it, because there were children being born every day. I didn't want to have children. I didn't really at that point want to have anything to do with boys. I couldn't see the attraction. I was only 13 or 14 then, and to me they all seemed very grubby and didn't have much going for them. It was later, when I was 15, that I got my first real crush and went steady for three months. Then he dumped me on my birthday. I carried the torch for him for a good year and a half afterwards. Nobody else was quite the same.

My parents didn't mind me bringing boyfriends home. The house was always open. In fact, if I remember, boyfriends had to make an appearance before I was allowed to go out with them. There was none of this 'he's picking me up at the bottom of the drive' bit. I had guys queueing up because I was in the band. There was always this kind of admiration for me because there weren't any other girls in bands around. They had no idea what I was like personally, but they saw the image and they wanted to buy the image. I went through a stage where I was invited to loads of senior proms from towns all around, because guys wanted to say they'd got that girl with them who was in The Rebels. That was a real status thing and I played on it, though I don't think I was ever all that interested in the guys I could get easily, and I could also be quite cutting and cruel if I didn't like a guy.

Then there was this romantic streak I had, which was always for the guys I couldn't get. I think it came from the books I read in my early teens. *Gone With The Wind* was a big influence – you know, 'fiddle-dee-dee, tomorrow is another day' with Scarlet and her great passion for Ashley. I remember we – my friends and I – roamed around having these great passions. We'd have these terrible crushes on guys who, for some reason or other, were out of reach for us. This was pretty true for most of my contemporaries.

You'd never go out with a boy who didn't have a car, and very often you'd pick the boy because of the type of car he had. It was all image. But, as I've said, he was picking you the same way – for the image. Though having a car was more than just that – it was more than a status symbol. It was essential, because there weren't really any buses, so it was all Shank's pony or getting a car. You simply had to have a car and everybody did have one, though generally they didn't own it personally. You just had the use of the parental car. Everybody learnt to drive as soon as they possibly could. You could get your licence at 16 and you did. You'd take your test literally on your birthday or the day afterwards. Then came the battle about when your parents would actually let you take out their car on your own.

Most families had two cars, because we were actually 25 miles outside of Boston. All the fathers drove to work in Boston, and all the mothers had to have separate cars to do the shopping and take the kids to school and whatever.

So there would be two cars, and even if your parents went out on the weekend there was always one car you could have. The second car was mostly a VW Beetle – that was the really trendy one to have and everybody had them. It was also the cheapest second car you could get. The family car was a more luxurious car which, if you were lucky, you'd get to drive sometimes. Unfortunately my father had what I called the Melmobile. Now the Melmobile was a 1960 Buick Electra 225, which was custom-made. It had been left to him by a very elderly family friend, who always had to have a new car every year and this was his last car. It was absolutely spectacular, but unfortunately a bit old-fashioned. There was this huge machine with big fins at the back and tinted black windows – it looked like the Mafiamobile. It was instantly recognisable around town, and I was terribly embarrassed because it wasn't a new Cadillac or a new Buick, like everybody else's parents had. I preferred to be seen in my mother's VW.

Anyway, I was talking about boyfriends and going out with them in cars, driving around. I think my parents were quite happy about all that and they'd be quite happy to leave me alone in the house for hours on end with a boy. They seemed to trust me and never led me to think that anything could happen that shouldn't. Though I remember my grandmother felt differently. Once when my parents had gone away, when I was about 16 or 17, she was brought in to stay with me, and she told me that if ever I was in a car and had to sit on a boy's lap, I should put a fully folded newspaper between him and me because 'things happen to men, you know'. I thought this was a scream and I told all my friends, but I don't even think at the time I was totally aware of erections. I really don't think that I was, and we just thought what my grand-mother had said was a huge giggle. We never thought about somebody getting carried away. I suppose in a way what you'd call us now would be prick-teasers. I mean, we could be terribly provocative with our short skirts and going out wearing practically nothing, especially in the summer.

Of course, we didn't stay this naïve. When you went out with a guy, you came to sort of accept that he was going to try and go as far as he could, but generally that wasn't very far. You'd go out with somebody and you'd be 'parking'. Now 'parking' was after you'd been to your movie or been to the local McDonalds to have your shake and your BigMac – although I don't think they had BigMacs then, but they did have hamburgers and there were McDonalds. Then you'd go to some really nice place – the beach was a particular favourite – and you'd sit in the car and get it all steamy on the inside from passionate kissing. Then occasionally, after about twenty minutes or so, you'd feel a little hand move up your side and start to want to caress your breast. That was the cue for you to move the hand down again. So next the hand would move in the opposite direction and try to get up your skirt. You'd let it get so far, and then you'd move it and put it some place where it couldn't do any harm at all. You'd let all this go on for about fifteen minutes and then you'd say, 'I think it's time I got home now.' Then the guy would take you home and you could see that there'd be a look of frustration in his eyes, but he would never really push things further.

No one ever asked me in my teen years to go all the way, because they knew what could happen. None of us, including the boys, wanted the responsibility of pregnancy. The Pill wasn't around then. It wasn't available for unmarried women until the very, very end of the sixties, and then only through a gynaecologist. There were no family planning clinics because everything in the States is private medicine, and you couldn't go to your family doctor and ask for the Pill because he would tell your parents. Your parents would be outraged. They certainly would never want you on the Pill and we didn't know much about condoms or diaphragms or anything like that. The boys never used condoms – they never got that far. If they did, nobody admitted it. Girls admitted to fooling around, being touched up, but nobody actually admitted to losing their virginity, because virginity was a thing you had to hang on to. It was your bargain for marriage. It was still very much a part of your upbringing in the sixties that a boy would not respect you if you had full sex with him. It was drummed into you that you must keep yourself 'pure' for matrimony. Besides, it was a small town where I lived and everybody knew everybody's business. You had your reputation to take care of. I only had to walk home from school with a boy and my mother would know before I was in the house, even if we'd parted at the end of the road.

There was one girl in my senior class in high school who got pregnant. That must have been in 1968, when I was 17. She was a girl in my fast stream and it was considered really shocking. My mother refused to let her in the house when we held our seminars there. She told me that if I hung around with such a girl, I'd get a bad reputation. This girl stayed in school until she was about six months' pregnant. Then she was sent away to a home for unwed mothers in Boston, and eventually came back and actually graduated with the class. She sat two rows to the back of me at the high school graduation and quipped as they were handing out the prizes, 'Where's my mother of the year award?' I didn't like her personally, but I thought she had tremendous guts to do that. The baby was adopted, of course. There was no way she would have been able to keep a child, but that was typical even in the late sixties. There were no such things in suburban communities as unwed mothers. Other girls also disappeared from school, apparently to go and live with relatives out of state. They either never appeared again, or they appeared after about a year and a half and everything was fine. In each case, no one was actually told what had happened, but they could make a good guess. What other logical reason was there for these girls to leave town so suddenly!

I'm sure things were different in places like San Francisco and the big cities, but remember I lived in small-town America where for the most part, if you wanted to have an easy life, you upheld the rules. Anyway, I never felt I was ready for sex then. Things only changed in the early seventies, once I went to university. Everybody was on the Pill by then. It became much easier to get hold of. I didn't go on the Pill until 1971, and I lost my virginity when I was 21 going on 22, which was beginning to be considered late. In fact, I started taking the Pill about six months before I lost my virginity, because I saw the absolute terror that my contemporaries were going through in the month after they'd lost their virginity, wondering, 'Am I? Am I not? Oh God, what have I done?' I'd see the tears and heartbreak of the ones who didn't make it – the ones who actually were pregnant. There wasn't any legal abortion in the States then. You had to come to England to have an abortion, and the richer families did send their daughters over here. There were also private clinics in Puerto Rico. I knew of a couple of girls who went there, but I vowed it would never happen to me. I would never be pregnant unless I wanted to be, and certainly not in a situation where I was on my own. I knew my parents would kill me.

Something else that didn't really hit small-town America until well into the seventies was the effect of the Gay Movement. In the sixties we – that is, my friends and I – weren't really aware of homosexuality except as a theoretical topic. It was something that we simply didn't recognise. To this day, I don't know if it was illegal in the States or not then. My parents had friends called Bob and Henry. Henry was definitely limp-wristed, as was my mother's hairdresser, which was something that she would comment on from time to time. Also, I remember referring to somebody once as being a bit queer and my mother snapping at me and saying, 'Don't you ever call anybody queer.' And I said, 'What do you mean? I meant queer as in peculiar.' And she said, 'No. It has a different connotation.' But she wouldn't explain. She just said, 'It has a different connotation and it's dangerous to refer to somebody as queer. If you think they're peculiar, you can say they're peculiar.'

After that, I can remember at one of the parties I went to, getting angry with a bunch of guys there. They were sitting separately from the girls and not really talking to us. Also, I fancied one of them like mad and I was very frustrated, because I had been trying for months and months to get him interested in me. So I blurted out, 'I think you're all queer.' By the way, we didn't know the term 'gay' then – that didn't come in till later. But anyway, I accused all these guys of being homosexual and, the funny thing was, that, of this particular bunch, quite a few of them did turn out to be homosexual – and they probably knew it at the time. One of them is still a great friend of mine. He later told me that he was inwardly terrified that I'd discovered his secret.

Homosexuality and sex in general were subjects that really were out of our depth. They certainly weren't something that boys and girls could discuss together. The only thing you ever said to a contemporary male on the subject of sex was 'No!' We were still basically very young and immature kids. The kind of things we'd get up to in the mixed groups I hung around with were pseudo-intellectual discussions and games. We had a good time. We used to go to the beach and run rampant at 3 o'clock in the morning, yelling and screaming quotations from Kafka, running into the sea. We thought we were absolutely wonderful – and everybody else probably found us totally insufferable. We used to talk about metaphysics and books we'd read and exhibitions. We also used to go into Boston to concerts and museums. We were terribly brattishly precocious. And we used to have parties every Friday and Saturday night, where we'd sit around talking and smoking dope.

The first time I did dope was when I was 17. I went with this friend of mine to a wildlife preserve, which was near his home. He had this pipe and this dope and said we were going to smoke it. We were so terrified that we were going to be discovered that every time we heard a twig break or a bird flutter, he'd want to put the pipe away, and I'd say, 'No, no, no, if we don't do this now, we'll never do it.' It was really a dare. We had to do it. We had to see what it was like. So we did it and he really got into it. He really liked it and did it quite a lot after that until he had a bad experience.

We were only ever into things like smoking hash – mari-
juana, never into anything 'hard' – though some of the
kids in the town from 1966 onwards were heavily into
LSD. I knew of a couple of guys who used to do LSD every
day for years. Now they're burnt-out wrecks – they've no
minds left. It was incredibly easy to get dope, much easier
than getting alcohol, because the legal drinking age in
Massachusetts was 21 and nobody of about 16 or 17 could
easily pass for 21. But everybody new somebody – an
older brother or sister at university or one of the artists
hanging around town – who could get hold of dope. The
town was on the coast. It was similar in some ways to a
Cornish fishing village, and there were a few artists and
other creative types living there, who'd probably been
smoking dope since the fifties. So you could always get
stuff if you knew where to go. I never heard of anybody
having any difficulty. You just asked around and somebody somehow got hold of some. I never had to actually
buy any. I've never bought any dope in my life, because it
was always there. But I only smoked occasionally, because
it was a social thing. It was *de rigueur* at one point – to
show you weren't stuffy, that you were contemporary.
Finally, when I got to university and got a bit older, I was
strong enough to admit I didn't really like it.

None of my group were ever really into the whole alternative culture thing, though. We may have smoked a bit of
dope, but that was all. The things that were happening in
a few of the cities or in England only reached us in a very
homogenised form. Don't forget that the States generally
at this point was probably about five years behind
England. There were pockets in places like New York, San
Francisco and Haight Ashbury that were really going to
town with the hippies and all the rest of the peace and love
bit, but we were never really into all that. We were part of
a rich, middle-class community. We saw ourselves as
college-bound for good careers. We were really insular. I
don't remember any of us even being interested in politics
or anything like that. You know, the first memory I have
of the Vietnam War was a friend of my father's who was a

real hawk – a 'hawk' was somebody who was very pro-Vietnam and a 'dove' was somebody who was definitely anti. I was about 16 at the time and I was in the car and this man said, 'Oh, I suppose like all students you're really a dove. You're really against the war.' And I can remember saying completely genuinely, 'I've never thought about it.'

Up to that point, the war was just something you saw on television and I didn't take in much that I saw on the news. All through the time when I was in school, I didn't actually know anybody who had been in Vietnam. Though one day I remember we didn't see a particular girl in school and we later learnt that her father, who was a professional soldier, had been killed in Vietnam. That was the first time anything about the war was ever brought home to me, so I'd hardly had a chance to think about whether I was for or against the war. I didn't decide about that until I went to university. I don't think my parents or their friends ever discussed Vietnam either, because they all would have been very pro the war. They were all people who had served in the Second World War and were quite militaristic. At that point, Massachusetts had a very strong Republican outlook, and so, if you were anything, you would be for the war.

The first time that I met anybody who'd been in Vietnam was when I was 16 and I'd gone on the trip to Florida I mentioned earlier, to visit my aunt and uncle in this geriatric trailer park. The people next door had some girls visiting them who were just slightly younger than me. These people were very generous and, because I was older and had a driving licence, they actually let me drive their car down to Miami one day with these girls. It was probably about 50 miles on the freeway. Anyway, we went to this very luxurious hotel and met this guy there, who had just come back from Vietnam. He was like a quadruple Purple Heart – he'd been shot all over the place. The thing that was stunning about him was that he was one of the most gorgeous people I'd ever met. He was about 19 and I was 16 and I thought, 'Wow!' He had this deep tan

and this blond hair, but he'd never take off his jeans. He
was never around in swimming trunks, the way everybody
else was, because it was his legs that had been shot up. He
came from the same area as I did and, when we were both
back home, I went out with him for a couple of months. It
never really worked, because he was so much older than I
was and wanted things that I wasn't capable of giving in a
relationship at that time. I was still too much of a school-
girl. He was already out working and doing things, and
he'd been in Vietnam – and had severe psychological
problems from it as well. He used to do a lot of drugs. At
that time, I didn't know that the guys in Vietnam did a lot
of drugs.

You could get drafted when you were 18, but it was
nearly always working-class boys. If you were a middle-
class kid of a good academic standard and could go to
university, chances are you wouldn't be drafted, which
was why I met so few people connected with Vietnam. It
was mainly the boys who unfortunately didn't come from
such a privileged background who were sent there, and
quite a few of them were black. Now the town I was
brought up in was entirely white. There weren't any black
people living there. The first time that I was aware of
black people in the town was when the town got a con-
science in my last year of school – 1967–8. They then got
together this programme where inner-city black kids
would come out to our school to have the benefit of this
marvellous middle-class education. They'd be bussed in
and they'd be bussed out again at the end of the day.
The programme was called something like TETCO and
we used to refer to these little black kids as TETCO
Americans.

There was quite a lot of controversy over this bussing
that was going on. I don't think anybody liked it. We felt
sorry for these black kids. Well, what kind of life were they
going to have? They'd come into this middle-class
community and get a very good academic education, but
they must have been exhausted by the time they got there
after an hour's bus ride from their inner-city ghettos. Then

in the afternoon they'd have to be taken off back, so they were not taking part in any sports or any extra-curricular activity. There was no real mixing or integration. If they hated us, I don't blame them. We were frankly quite cruel to them.

Black people, however, were generally removed from my course of activity, so I don't think I thought very much about racial issues – although I was aware of the racial conflict in America and of the whole Civil Rights Movement with Luther King. In fact, I think it scared us. We simply hadn't encountered blacks in our neighbourhoods, and so we had no way of gauging what these people – and we did definitely see them as being almost a different kind of species – wanted. I sometimes felt that maybe I ought to get to know somebody who was black and see what they were like, but I didn't think about it a lot, because I just didn't run into black people very often. Even in my classes at Boston University I don't remember any blacks. There were blacks on campus, but they were doing other things like Afro-American studies. They really kept together and kept separate. In the Students' Union there was a big canteen and they kept to their own tables. If you happened to sit at one of their tables by mistake, everything would go quiet and you'd know to leave. Even if you just walked past a group of blacks who were talking, they'd go quiet. In a way, you really felt that to them you were the enemy and that they were the enemy to you.

When they had black girls in the university, they put them all together in the student halls of residence. There was no effort at all made at integration. All the black girls would be together and all the white girls would be together. You might see one of these black girls who lived in a room down the corridor and you'd nod and she might nod and say 'hello', but I don't remember ever having a single conversation with a black girl. We were a bit wary of each other. We'd circle around each other. They were looking for prejudice in us and we were looking for strange behaviour in them, because we'd heard they were very militant. I was scared to death that one would take a knife to me, although rationally I realised that that was crazy.

I just wasn't familiar enough with black people. As I said, my school and my community had been all white. I saw blacks in films and on television, but all I knew about them from those was either the 'Yez sir!' or the Big Momma thing – blacks being shown in a subservient role. Of course, I also saw black people when I went into the city – on buses or walking past me in the streets. But then they were in their own communities, going about their own business, and I just felt it was all nothing to do with me. I wouldn't have said I was prejudiced. Intellectually, I felt that any kind of prejudice was wrong, but emotionally I just couldn't deal with this 'species', because I'd never really had to. They were as weird to me as the King of Siam, and when I did encounter racial issues, I just felt perplexed.

I'd heard of race riots and stuff to do with the Klan, but again it was all television stuff to me and quite a lot of what I saw on television had an air of unreality about it. Vietnam was the same – totally unreal. They'd show pictures on the news and you'd be sitting there watching them and maybe reading a paper or a book at the same time. You saw so much violence on television anyway, that it was often very hard to discriminate between something that was really happening and something that was fiction-alised. Also, my life at the time was going along in such an ordered fashion that I thought I knew where I slotted into society and couldn't really relate a lot of the violence and social unrest that I saw on television to my own world. Nobody was coming after me with knives. I knew about rape and I knew about mugging, but it was something that happened to other people. I still thought it was relatively safe. I used to hitch-hike. When I was at university, my hall of residence was probably a couple of miles from where I attended classes, and I thought nothing of sticking up my thumb and getting into a car with someone. We all did it. Nothing ever happened. It was only later on that we realised what a tremendous risk we had been taking.

I did get caught up in a riot once at Harvard. I think

this was in 1969. I was over there going to a library and when I came out of the library, there was this huge riot going on. I just ducked down a back street and ran like hell till I got to a quiet neighbourhood. I didn't know where I was, but I kept on walking till I found a bus and just got on it and left. However, even that didn't really terrify me and it was about the only time I came close to anything like it. I was never involved in student demonstrations or unrest. I just wasn't very politically or socially conscious. All the times when people around me were in tremendous turmoil and felt very strongly about issues, I could only really see what they were talking about from an academic point of view. Also, my father had told me if I was ever involved in a student demonstration, I would have my money cut off and would have to quit university, and then what would I do? I thought that would mean I'd end up as a shop assistant in Woolworth's, and I didn't want that, did I!

There were a lot of left-wing agitators at the time when I was at university and, although I didn't take part in anything political at all, I was definitely aware of what was going on. You'd see violence, you'd see demonstrations. I'm not sure now what year Kent State was, but I think it was the springtime of my first or maybe even my second year at university, and I can remember being told what had happened. We were all told about it. It was about two weeks before term was supposed to end and we were asked to get out of the university and go home. Because Kent State had happened, they closed down Boston University. They must have been frightened that the same kind of thing could happen there. None of us had any final exams that year. Instead, we were graded on what we'd done on our courses so far. But even the courses had been very disrupted, because about every other day there had been a bomb threat. I can remember one course I was doing in philosophy. I only attended about three lectures and that wasn't because I was skipping class. It was because every time I went to the class in this particular building, there'd be a bomb scare by the Weathermen, part of SDS –

Students for a Democratic Society – or one of the other really hard-core agitating left-wing groups. We weren't allowed into the building because they didn't know whether there was a bomb or not. As it turned out, there never were any bombs, and a rumour soon started going around that these bomb threats were actually being made by some students who were not political at all, but were afraid of failing their exams.

Boston was a very political university. The students were never as well organised as in, say, somewhere like Columbia, but the student population was big and a large percentage of that was actively left-wing. Remember, it was a very volatile time politically. This was the time of the Civil Rights Movement and Boston had a strong element of black students, because, like a lot of universities at the time, it had been actively recruiting them to redress the balance. It was also the time of Bobby Kennedy running for President and being assassinated. If you wanted to be interested in politics, it was definitely the time to be there, because there were always spaces you could fit into. Political agitation was a very social thing. The most dynamic people were involved in politics. However, I was just interested in rock 'n' roll. While everybody was out demonstrating, I was seeing every single group that came into town.

I didn't think about big social or world issues. I was very closed in. I just wanted to become rich and famous and gave no thought as to how or why I was going to become rich and famous. I just thought that if I was talented enough, then somehow doors were going to open. At the end of university, when people were applying for jobs and things, it never crossed my mind to do the same. I just thought when the time came, I'd knock on the door and the door would open and I'd walk in and I'd be so good at what I did, that the riches and fame would just naturally follow. The same applied to getting married. I simply thought that when I came to the proper age, that the 'knight on the white charger' would appear and I'd just go off with him and be happy ever after. I never thought as far as how I was actually going to make my daily crust, or where I was going to meet this man, or what he would do for a living. When I think of it now, I think, 'God, what a sucker you were, what a softy! How come you didn't put all of that together?' I think the reason why I didn't was because these were things that nobody ever gave the slightest thought to in my social group. We naturally assumed that we would do well because we were bright and because we were from the right background, and that if we played our cards right – though nobody ever told us exactly what cards – nothing bad could happen.

My parents never discussed my future. They never talked about what I might like to do. I think like me they just assumed I'd go to university, get a good job or something, and probably get married, though not necessarily in that order. Also, I don't think it made that much difference to them that I was a girl. It wasn't that they were interested in women's rights, but that being an only child I wasn't being brought up with the traditional female stereotyping you get with a girl when there are brothers around. I never had to help with the housework. For my pocket money I maybe had to mow the lawn or wash the car, but I wasn't being slotted into a particularly female role. I was never told that anything was beyond me. However, I wasn't obviously being told I could do anything I wanted to either, and my father always made it clear that he didn't want my mother to go out to work. When I asked him about this, he gave the really lame excuse that he didn't want his tax bracket to go up. But we knew that he really didn't want his standing in the community to go down by having a working wife, as people might think he couldn't support her and me. That really is what people thought at the time.

I wasn't very aware of prejudice against women while I was still at school. I had no idea, until probably about the time I went to university, that women at one point actually didn't have the vote. I suppose where I first noticed prejudice against women was when I applied for vacation jobs. Because I have a man's name, people would often assume that I was a boy. So I'd get accepted for interviews and then when I walked in it would all change. I can remember this one interview I went to, which was in 1969. It was to work at a radio station and the man who interviewed me looked at me and said, totally flummoxed, 'Now, what's a nice little girl like you want with a great big job like this?' The job was a kind of student apprenticeship as an announcer, just doing continuity sort of things, but he'd expected that it was going to be for a man. I looked at him and noticed that he had on a badly fitting toupee which was crooked, and I was dying to say to him, 'By the way, your toupee is on crooked,' and blow him a huge raspberry, but I was too well brought up to be rude. Instead, I just said, 'Nothing, thanks,' and turned on my heels and left. He'd really infuriated me.

Later I did end up getting a student job at the local public broadcasting service radio station as a one-day-a-week news announcer. It was part of the graduate programme and I was the only undergraduate accepted on it. It was a very highly thought-of position and I did it very well. If I had wanted to have a job there after I had got out of university, it possibly would have been open to me because I had done so well, though, if I remember, you didn't really have at that point any female newscasters. Instead, you always had your father figures, the Walter Cronkites, the grey-haired men who'd get up there and tell you the news in a very strong authoritative tone, and you would take whatever they said as being gospel. Women only tended to be on radio or television then as authorities on female subjects. They hadn't yet crossed any divide.

Girls were usually told then that they had to learn to type if they wanted to get a job. I suppose it's still the same. But anyway, I just thought that didn't apply to me. I was bright and I would have been to university, so why should I be somebody's typist? In fact, when I came out of university and went to any kind of an employment agency or to anybody for a job, the first thing they asked me was 'Can you type?' Every single girl I knew, no matter where she ended up, started off typing. No matter how good a degree she had, no matter how many letters she had after her name, she still ended up behind that damned keyboard and she still ended up making the tea and the coffee. Despite the fact that this was a time when several very forceful figures, like Gloria Steinem and Betty Friedan, were fighting to promote women's rights, equality was still seen as a joke by the majority of the male population. If you admitted to a man that you were 'one of those women's libbers', you'd probably end up involved in a 45-minute argument, trying to justify everything and still getting nowhere. So for the most part, women learnt that it was better not to mention the subject if they wanted to get anywhere or get what they wanted. They learnt to keep their thoughts to themselves and their mouths shut.

However, I was only 19 going on 20 at the end of the sixties and I was still very unformed. A lot of the new issues had touched me in some ways, but in others I was still very traditional. All I really wanted were nice clothes, untold riches and fame, and a romantic boyfriend. I basically wanted the white tower and all the knights out front dancing attendance to me, and I wasn't the only one who felt this way. The only thing I knew about being assertive with men was in saying 'no'. When it came to sex, you were definitely brought up to be assertive – you said no all the time and you said no fairly forcibly. But even then, you didn't have to be that forceful about it until the late sixties. That was when the boys started to say on the first date, 'Well, obviously you have a psychological problem. You're uptight if you're not going to go to bed with me.' Suddenly the whole thing became really difficult.

At university we used to sit in the halls of residence at night and there would always be two or three girls in tears because they'd lost their virginity that week and were wondering whether they were going to get their 'friend' that month or not. Changes in the halls of residence rules about that time – this was about 1968 to 1969 – didn't help either. In fact, they reflect how much general social attitudes changed in the late sixties. In my first year at university no males, not even fathers, were allowed

upstairs in the female halls of residence, but by 1969 everything changed. You could suddenly have anybody in at
any time, and in a way it was good because it allowed us
the freedom to develop relationships. But in a way it was
bad, because it put girls under a real pressure to have sex.
The opportunity was now there, because you had the place
to have it. You could no longer say to a guy, 'No, you can't
come up. Those are the rules.' Also, there was everything
in the papers about how this was the time of sexual liberation. But we were young and a lot of us weren't ready for
it. There were very few who were naturally promiscuous.
Most girls who ended up having sex without being psycho-
logically prepared ended up in a terrible emotional
dilemma about it, because they saw that they had traded
away their 'big gift'. That's the way most of us still
thought of our virginity then. It was your big gift to be
surrendered on your marriage bed. Sex was probably
permissible if you were engaged to be married, but other
than that you felt you should really hold off.

We had this basic mushiness. With the free love and
free sex attitude and the liberation that was being touted
in the media to us, I think a lot of younger women felt
really uncomfortable with their own emotions – certainly
I did. We were attracted to all the new things that
were happening. We wanted the ability to expand
ourselves and have a good time, but at the same time we
wanted commitment. That's the way we'd been brought
up. We didn't necessarily want a husband and children
straight out of university, but that was probably what
most of us saw at the end of the road. Not that we were all
looking for the perfect executive husband. That idea had
really gone out the window by then. Nobody I knew particularly wanted that. We didn't want to live in somebody
else's shadow, being kept back in our earning potential by
somebody else's salary and status. But we did want somebody – somebody more exciting possibly, perhaps with an
artistic bent.

There were girls who were going around and saying,
'Yeah, I'm free,' and dropping out and becoming hippies,

but they soon came a cropper. Most of them found that they couldn't really make enough money to support their lifestyles and they were having to take badly paid jobs in restaurants or shops, and the guys who they were with, who had been so keen to get them on this road, soon lost interest. So there they were, having given up university to live with some guy, because that was considered the trendy, liberated thing to do, and they'd end up with somebody who wasn't particularly interested in working – so they had to earn all the money – and somebody who was more interested in smoking dope than in them. They'd be going out to work in these appalling fast-food joints just to make the money to pay the rent. I had several friends like that. Ultimately, we lost contact, because they became embarrassed to see me – and I became slightly embarrassed to see them as well.

But even if I didn't get involved with radical politics or sexual liberation and all that, I wasn't completely cut off from all the changes that were going on. I didn't just accept my parents' Protestant work ethic, which was really quite Thatcherite. They believed that you only got what you worked for and you didn't ask anybody for anything, you didn't get into debt, you saved your money, and you never bought anything unless you could put cash on the line. The society they moved in was really terribly formal – you had a public face and you kept your private thoughts to yourself. Even in the late sixties, I think most people still felt like that, because that was the way they had been brought up. Even younger people felt uncomfortable with all the 'peace and love', 'hang loose', 'let it be' bit. Most people, in fact, wanted their boundaries. They made them feel safe.

Take something like the Manson case. That really shook America in the sense that people had been gradually getting more freedom and more money and more equality, and what was the result? You got this wholesale massive slaughter. Also, it had happened to people who were privileged and famous, so if it could happen to people like that, nobody felt safe any more. Now in a way this had been happening since the early sixties. There had been this increasing violence, first with Kennedy dying, then his brother being assassinated as well, and Luther King and the student riots and the race riots, and cities and neighbourhoods generally getting more dangerous places to live. The intimation was that if you pushed the boundaries back too far, you'd get a backlash.

JULIA

I was 4 when the sixties started, and some of my earliest clear memories are of things that are archetypically sixties. For instance, one of the first pop records I remember is *She Loves You, yeah, yeah, yeah.* I can remember hearing it and telling my mother that I thought the words were really, really boring and being quite snobby about it. I can also remember having Twist records and getting up very early on a Sunday and learning to do the Twist to hits like *Twist and Shout.* That must have been in 1963, or maybe even earlier than that – perhaps it was 1961. Also, I can remember Kennedy being assassinated. But probably the start of the sixties for me was marked by moving down to Bristol. My parents were from the North. They got married very young because my mother was pregnant with me, and split up when I was about 4. My mother and I then moved down from this small town near Manchester to Bristol. She got a flat in one of those large Georgian houses in Clifton and got herself a job at the BBC.

So right at the beginning of the sixties my mother made this break. She moved away from the very traditional lower-middle-class Methodist community that she had been brought up in, to Bristol, which was starting to be extremely lively. Suddenly she was going to lots of parties for the first time and meeting lots of people. She was involved in lots of things that the sixties were all about. There were a lot of young, unattached, creative people around Clifton at the time, and I don't think it was any problem for her being a single parent with a young baby. She had moved herself into a milieu where it was accept-able, and she made a lot of friends, who simply thought her exciting and admirable for having done this rather brave thing of getting out of her marriage and starting out on her own. She was in an environment where she could live in the way that she wanted to. In fact, I think where we lived was a bit of a haven for single-parent families. If I remember, two of our neighbours were single mothers and I don't think childcare was a problem. I went to a state nursery and there were always plenty of people around to babysit.

I never thought that it was particularly strange that I didn't have a dad around. We moved in a circle where there were lots of people who weren't part of a regular family. As I've said, two women living right next door to us were on their own with small children, and I had a friend about my age who also didn't live with her father. So I didn't really feel an oddity, though I think I was aware that I was very dependent on my mother and very, very close to her. When I got older, I became more aware of being different from a lot of children I knew. When I was about 10, I was really very conscious of the fact that the man my mother was now married to wasn't my father and things like that. I became very sensitive about it.

What I was aware of from very early on was that I was rather separate from the mainstream – the more traditional – home life of lots of children. I doubt if many of the children I went to school with had mothers who were leading the kind of life my mother did, going to parties and all that. My mother had rebelled against her upbringing and against her marriage, which had broken up because my father had gone off with somebody else. I mean, she had come from a very nice, but quite strict lower-middle-class household, where her father wouldn't let her mother work because he was ashamed of it and gave her very little freedom and so forth. I think she'd had enough of it, so she rebelled against it all, which in fact was very much in tune with a lot of the things that the sixties were supposed to be about – kicking at the establishment, at repression, and trying to find a freer, more open, way to live.

Then David came along. At first they just lived together, which I don't think I found at all odd. In fact, I don't think I ever thought about it. All I can remember is just being very suspicious of this new person who was taking up so much of my mother's time. One incident that was quite funny about the time when they were just living together was that they would get post addressing them both by three different names – either by my mother's maiden name, or by David's surname, or sometimes by both their surnames hyphenated. Now the woman who lived in the flat upstairs was a sort of maiden-aunt type of great sobriety, and she used to sort their mail into three different piles according to the name on the envelope, just to make the point that she knew perfectly well that they were 'living in sin'.

However, they did get married when I was 6. I think that was in 1962, just after that very severe winter. At first I was very wary of my stepfather, but I think I was very wary of all men, because of not seeing much of my own father when I was very young, which had made me feel rejected by him. I think that did affect me more than I realised at the time. But David did make big efforts to woo me. I can remember him buying me presents. Once he bought me these pale pink and blue mittens. He was like that, very conscious of trying to win me over. But I was still very wary of him. I think I was quite a shy and closed-in little girl. As soon as I could read, I used to spend a lot of time on my own with my books or just playing.

Once they were married, life did seem to become more orderly, although they were both rather trendy and we moved around a lot because of my stepfather's job. Throughout the sixties we moved probably once a year on average, and I went to about twelve schools altogether. But everything did seem quite stable, perhaps because we were living in small provincial towns where very little was going on. Almost immediately after they married we moved down to Dorset, as David got a job down there. At first we lived in a really pretty house in the countryside. Then we moved to Weymouth, where we actually bought a house. Before that, it had always been renting.

We stayed in the house in Weymouth for quite a while really. It was probably a couple of years that we were there, which was a long time then for us to be in one place. It was a typical semi-detached in a nice street with a medium-sized garden, very suburban, very nice, and quite sort of old-fashioned and traditional inside. But as soon as they arrived there, David and my mother decided to transform the place completely. They ripped out all the inside walls downstairs and had black and white tiles put in through from the hallway into the back. The whole kitchen was done out with pine and those copper strips that went all along the bottom of the units. There was an old pantry and a sort of dining-room – these were knocked out and they created this huge living-room with a big beam across. It was completely open to the hall and had an expanse of rush matting, which then was the latest thing. All the walls were white. The old-fashioned tile fireplace came out to give a hole in the wall with a stainless steel strip around it. I think there was a rocking chair in there. Then there were shelves in the alcoves with the stereo – or record player as you would have called it then – on, and there was a studio couch that could be turned into a bed and a table and chairs in one corner. It was very, very sixties, that room. They installed oil-fired central heating, because with David then working for Shell they could get oil cheap. Remember, this was pre-oil crisis days. You can't imagine anyone doing that now, whether they worked for Shell or not! And the irony is that they did all that and it ended up looking immaculate – you know, all *Homes and Gardens* – but then we moved out and sold it to somebody who put all the walls back in and turned it back into the traditional semi we had had in the first place.

Dorset isn't exactly a 'swinging' place and we must have stood out a bit from our neighbours. I think I thought that we were something special. Although when I went into the houses of friends at school, I didn't just think they were stuffy and boring. In fact, I thought their houses were terribly safe and nice, just like I'd read about in books. You know, part of me really hungered to be in what I thought of as an ordinary family. But we did have some 'trendy' neighbours. I can remember one couple who lived up the road from us, this woman called Celia who was a friend of my mother's and Duncan, her husband. I've got this amazing photograph of my mother and Celia, lounging around on the floor. They were having a spaghetti party and they were wearing caftans. They were trying so hard to be trendy and yet there they were in a suburban street in Dorset. It was sort of ironic really. I can remember Duncan and Celia having this Mini, and they took a cine film of all these people getting into the Mini and getting out the other side. It looked as if there were twenty people in the Mini. There was a shot of the Mini being driven off down the road with legs and arms coming out on all sides.

My mother was about 28 when we were living in this place in Weymouth, and David must have been about 25 or 26. He was ambitious and full of grand ideas. I also had one baby brother by now, Thomas, who is seven years younger than me. He was born in the house in Weymouth. Both my brothers were born at home. My mother was very keen on that. She had had me in an old-fashioned hospital near Manchester, where she'd got the whole works, being shaved and kept in for a whole week, and she said it was horrible. I think that's why she felt so strongly about having her other children at home. Also, there was a big move towards home confinement and natural childbirth in the early to mid-sixties, and we had a good midwifery service. I think women were actually quite encouraged to have their babies at home. They only insisted that first babies were delivered in hospital. It's funny the way the emphasis has changed rather.

David's father came to live with us for a while in that house too. He was a very nice old man whose wife had died of a stroke, and he had finally been made redundant after God-knows-how-many years. Later, David's brother also moved in. He was in his very early twenties and played in a group that was just like The Beatles. They did the kind of things The Beatles had done. They went off to Hamburg and the whole works. I thought he was the bee's knees. He had a Beatles haircut and he used to go around wearing black trousers and a black polo-necked shirt and winkle-pickers. When he wasn't playing in the band, he was an electrical engineer. He had this bedroom that was entirely carpeted with the insides of televisions. It was a complete tip with clothes always all over the floor. He'd arrive and work for a while, but then suddenly he'd be off with the band somewhere else. He actually made a few records and I thought he was really very trendy indeed. He was a nice chap. He now sells recording equipment, makes stacks of money, and goes off to Japan all the time. I haven't seen him for years and years and years.

Our next move came when David got a job near Northampton. We rented part of this old farmhouse out in the countryside. That was a really nice place for me. I was very sorry to leave Weymouth and especially to leave our house, which I was fond of, but it was fun living on the farm. The only problem was that I had to go to this small country school, which was full of kids who thought I was completely off the wall. I was teased mercilessly for having what they thought of as a posh accent, and they were really horrid to me because I read books and was not very good at sports and things like that. I really felt like a fish out of water, and I think my mother probably did a bit too. She was used to having more people around, but again she managed to find all these eccentrics who were living in the countryside. We knew one couple, the wife was French, and they lived in a converted, spruced-up cottage with an Aga in it and she baked these incredibly delicious chocolate cakes. In retrospect, I suspect that David was having an affair with her. Then we knew another family who lived quite near us, also in a farmhouse, and they kept all these eccentric animals. They had a donkey and these strange Chinese goats, and funny ducks and hens and things like that. All these types were really 'refugees' from the city. They were the people who couldn't quite cope with London and other big cities in the 'swinging sixties', but were trying to do something about it in another way by sort of dropping out. I suppose they were a bit like the hippies, but before the hippy thing really started.

Even with these people around, I think my mother still felt very isolated. She had worked for a while when we were in Dorset, but now she had two very small boys – my second brother Paul was born when we were in Northampton – and I was still pretty young. It would have been difficult to tie all that up with any kind of job, though I don't think David was one of those men who disliked his wife working. He was into women being independent in a certain way. I think he liked women who would stand up to him a bit, although he was really very sexist too. For one thing, he was completely obsessed with women being really thin. I mean, talk about Twiggy culture – I remember my mother dieting and starving herself to get back into a bikini only three weeks after she had had Thomas. He was always going on about how she should lose weight and be thinner. I think all that had a profound effect on me later, when I rebelled against the sort of attitude he had. I hated him treating my mother like that. I was very protective of her and also very resistant to him having any authority over me.

I can remember having a great row with David over him trying to make me do something or other, and me refusing and telling him he wasn't my father and how dare he order me around. He was quite a moody man. He could be charming if he chose to be, but he wasn't easy to live with. He was very selfish. He worked very hard and was quite preoccupied, although he was good with children. He would play with us and so forth and take us out on extravagant little outings, but he was never really good at day-to-day family life. When he felt like it, he could be very sentimental and make a big fuss about how he liked being a father, but only when he felt like it. If you made demands on him when he wasn't in the mood, then he would just be really cross with you. I think he got away with a lot, and after a while he started being unfaithful.

David is a bit of a philanderer by nature, but the whole sixties atmosphere sort of exaggerated that side of him. All that business about 'free love' and the 'sexual revolution' meant that there were more opportunities for things like that. However, I wasn't really aware of his affairs and that things were not well between him and my mother until I was about 9 or 10. Then I started to notice the odd thing, though generally they were very discreet about their disagreements. My mother at least certainly tried hard to maintain a nice home atmosphere.

We were only in Northampton for about nine months. Then we moved back to the coast. David was trying to start up his own business and, with three children and my mother not working, we were pretty broke. This time we rented a house and most of the money went into the business. There were few parties and I can't remember my parents having much of a social life. Things got worse between David and my mother, and eventually in 1967 they separated. I must have been 11 at the time. We moved back to Bristol into a very similar circle to the one we'd mixed in when we'd lived there before. We got a flat on Whiteladies Road and it became somewhere where lots of people dropped in. My mother joined a poetry circle, and later on got a job at a boys' school. She used to invite all these sixth-form boys round on Friday nights to discuss poetry. My friends thought it was amazing!

I can remember feeling a bit in awe of these sixth-form boys, though later on I actually went out with two of them. One was rather a poseur who wore very tight purple flared trousers and had long straight black hair, which he used to flick back in the same way that Mick Jagger used to flick his hair. He was very scornful of the adult world, and wrote an extraordinarily bad rebellious sort of poetry that didn't rhyme or anything. But he had a scooter, which was quite a status symbol then because nobody else had any transport, so I went out with him. He took me to see the Velvet Underground at the Bristol Union. That must have been right at the end of the sixties, when I was 14. It was pretty much my first date. I can remember borrowing some of my mother's clothes for it. My mother always wore fashionable clothes like stretch pants with stirrups, and big sloppy-joe sweaters and then mini-skirts. She didn't wear them as short as I wore them, but she definitely wore mini-skirts, and she had a caftan and other really fashionable clothes. My friends used to be amazed that she wore these things and that I could borrow them for parties. When maxis came in, she had this wonderful full-length red coat that buttoned all the way down. I thought it was stunning. I wore that too.

I started becoming interested in clothes soon after we moved back to Bristol, but we didn't have that much money, so I could only have very few things. When I was 13 I was actually given an allowance, a monthly allowance, and I had to buy my own clothes out of this. It was part of the maintenance that my mother had arranged with David. He paid it directly to me and my brothers but, because his employment was very erratic, the money often didn't come. So I didn't have very many clothes, although the things I had were quite trendy. I can remember having a dress that was bright yellow and sort of like a string vest with very small holes. I can remember wearing that with a body stocking underneath it, and being quite unaware of the sort of impact that I was having by wearing something so revealing and outrageous. When I was younger, I also used to wear brightly coloured tights with polo-necked sweaters. I had this bottle-green ribbed tights and polo-necked sweater outfit that I used to wear without a skirt or anything. That was very sixties, I suppose.

I started experimenting with make-up too when I was about 13. I used to wear bright-yellow nail varnish and yellow lipstick, which must have looked disgusting. Then I had a sort of purple lipstick which was in at the time – from Biba. But I didn't really get into wearing skin make-up and the more professional look. I was into rather hippy things like face painting. I had Mary Quant face paints, and can remember one of my boyfriends painting my face and then going to a photo booth to take pictures of it.

When the Vidal Sassoon geometric cut came in, some of the girls I knew had it, but I didn't particularly want it myself. I can remember desperately wanting to have long, blonde straight hair like 'the Shrimp' [Jean Shrimpton]. Instead, I had long, very curly, frizzy hair and used to wear yellow velvet ribbons tied around it squaw-style. Our form mistress used to hate this and go quite spare with me. Also, because I had been to so many different schools and my mother couldn't afford to buy me a completely new uniform for each one, I never wore quite the correct things, and this was a source of annoyance too. I started out at my school in Bristol wearing a grey pleated skirt and a black and yellow striped tie, when the actual uniform was navy and yellow. So I always looked odd and I sometimes used to really envy these two friends I had. They were both about 5′ 2″ and very neat, and had the sort of mothers who pressed their clothes for them. They always arrived looking terribly nicely turned out. One of them was blonde and very pretty, and in a way I was terribly envious of them. I was already very tall and gangly with this unruly mass of frizzy hair and these odd clothes. The only advantage I had was that I was very skinny and everybody used to call me 'Twiggy' and tell me that I should be a model. Also, I had a reputation for being trendy out of school, which I quite liked. I used to walk around without any shoes on, like Sandie Shaw, and wear incredibly short skirts, real bum-freezers, even when I was still only 12.

My mother never really questioned what I wore, although she must have sometimes worried a bit about the length of my skirts and some of the more provocative clothes. But I think because she had had such a lot of parental interference when she was a teenager, she was very consciously holding back and trying as much as possible to let me do what I wanted. She was always very sensible about telling me about things like boys and sex and contraception. I was given a 'how you were born' record when I was about 8. It was a record that told you the facts of life, all very proper and narrated in this very English voice. Sex wasn't something that was hush-hush in our household, and we occasionally had conversations about it. My mother's line was always that you should wait until you found someone you really cared about before you did it and, because she was relatively open, I think I was quite sensible.

I knew about the Pill and where I could get it, although I didn't go on it until I was 16. Also, I was told about periods when I was quite young, and it was always assumed that when I started I would use tampons and not horrible old-fashioned sanitary towels. When she was young my mother had hated having periods, because they couldn't even afford sanitary towels and just used rags. She told me it was horrible and sordid and that she had hated it. She thought that tampons were a brilliant invention and she also taught me to use Lil-lets rather than Tampax. 'You don't want to stuff those bits of cardboard up you,' she said. She had a very down-to-earth, straightforward attitude towards these things.

Except there were some taboos. I can remember once I'd left this box of Lil-lets in a toilet bag in the bathroom, all open so you could see there were lots of tampons in it, and she was really embarrassed, because we had a male lodger at the time. So although to me she was very open, I did take in the lesson that periods were the sort of thing you weren't supposed to talk to boys or men about. Is it *The Female Eunuch* that has this thing about how a truly liberated woman will suck her own menstrual blood off her lover's penis? I now think of that as a typical piece of sixties garbage, but then it was the sort of thing that some people would go on about and do! I suppose the intention behind it all was good. It was all part of the sexual liberation thing, striving for more honesty and openness. Even just talking about it meant breaking through some of the taboos that were still around.

However, the whole of adult society at the time seemed to me to be obsessed with sex. I was allowed to stay up quite a bit and I used to sit around and listen to grown-ups talking. They seemed to talk about sex an awful lot and it all seemed so boring and so sordid. Then, at 13 or 14 when I started to wear these rather provocative clothes and was fashionably tall and very slim and beginning to look like a woman, I was really quite startled at the effect I could have on men. I'd go to parties and these 35-year-olds wanted to dance with me and paw me. It gave me a real feeling of power to think that, just by wearing these clothes, blokes would think that I was something interesting. Yet their reaction also made me very angry. I hated the way that women generally were treated as sex objects and controlled by men.

There was a lot of propaganda in the sixties about how it was now supposed to be OK for girls to have lots of affairs and sleep around with different boyfriends. It was only later on, when I had done that for a bit, that I realised how much that worked against women and only really gave them the freedom to be more thoroughly abused by men. Despite my initial wariness of boys, I started going out with them when I was much too young and for all the wrong reasons. It was what my friends were doing and I wanted to fit in. If I had behaved as I really wanted to, I think I would have been regarded as a freak, but I might have been happier in myself because I wouldn't have been acting out what to me was a charade. I think I really wanted to spend more time reading and studying, and I think I would have discovered an awful lot earlier that I was a lesbian.

Peer pressure also made me let my academic work slide. I went to a mixed grammar school when I was 11 and when I first went there I worked really hard. But I was teased heavily for it, particularly by the boys, and I had hardly any friends. I remember walking into an art class one day and all the boys chanting 'Flat as a pancake, flat as a pancake!' because I hadn't started to develop very much then. The boys used to really tease me about that and the fact that I wore glasses as well. Most of the girls kept away from me, too. Perhaps I threatened them by being clever. Then a couple of girls in my class made friends with me and that changed things a lot. I felt much more accepted and they took me out to the local club. I got involved in the social life and started going out instead of studying. We talked about boys and records and clothes and I found it all quite boring, but it meant that I was accepted and had friends. I made a real trade-off. I decided that I was going to stop being clever in order to be accepted. I suppose I was giving in to the traditional idea that it isn't feminine to be clever.

Perhaps things would have been different at an all-girls school, but it's only quite recently that people have started realising that single-sex education is actually better for girls. At the time, the popular liberal view was that mixed education was preferable. My mother was a Labour voter and definitely into such ideas. She believed strongly in state schools and mixed education, so I think that she much preferred me to go to a co-educational school. Anyway, I'm not sure if there was a single-sex school that I could have gone to and my grammar school was really very good. It had been established about five years before I went there from the amalgamation of a boys' grammar and girls' high, both of which were quite old. It was an excellent school. It was very forward thinking. They did Nuffield science, modern maths and all that kind of thing, which for 1967 was really in the forefront. However, I think I can remember doing some modern maths earlier on when I was still in primary school. It must have been just beginning then and they actually had sessions on it for parents in the evenings to come and find out how it worked and how they could understand it. I did go to some very good schools.

At home I had the example of a fairly independent capable mother. Even when she and David were together, she was always the one who organised things and I was particularly aware of that when they split up. All through my adolescent years, when I started thinking about role models and trying to think about what I wanted to be, I was very aware of her running the household, managing on a minute budget and making everything happen. I don't think I was treated differently from my brothers, but of course they were a lot younger than me so I was helping my mother with household things when they were still too young for all that. From when I was 13, it was my job to take the laundry to the laundrette and I used to help with the cooking and do lots of babysitting – my brothers were still only very small then. But I don't think I was pressurised into doing any of this. Quite frankly, I think I did it because my mother was on her own at the time and needed help, and partly because I was quite mature for my age. I think I was fairly adult and responsible and identified quite a lot with my mother. She was still relatively young. She was going out to parties and doing some of the kinds of things that I was starting to do, so it wasn't much like a mother–daughter relationship. It was more like older and younger sister. We were very friendly to each other in lots of ways.

I think towards the end of the sixties I gradually became aware of the women's movement that was starting up then. It was the sort of thing my mother would talk about and I think I was always very alert to any signs of change in the status of women. Also, because my mother had done so much on her own, I really didn't have the idea that I needed to find myself a man in order for my life to succeed. Throughout my adolescence I said that I would never get married and that I would never have children. Until I was about 17, I thought that being a wife was a terrible career and that it wasn't something that I wanted to do. I think my experience of my father and stepfather had made me very cynical about marriage and about men. When I did eventually say that I might get married, I made it very clear that I didn't want ever to get divorced and that therefore I would only marry if I was absolutely sure that it would be for good. But I never thought that if I did get married that I wouldn't have a career. I think a lot of girls then were beginning to think it was possible to reconcile getting married and having a family with doing a job.

Now that I think back, I suppose I did assume that if you had children you would take time off when they were very young, at least until they could go to nursery school. I was simply basing all this on my mother's experience. She was at home for a substantial period of time when I was young, and later nursery-school places had always been available for us. I therefore assumed that it would be easy to take two or three years off from a career. But I did think that I was not going to get married until I was ready for it, assuming that that would be something like the positively ancient age of 25 or 30, when I would have had time to build up a career. Yes, 30 did seem terribly, terribly old, especially as there was such a lot of publicity then about people in their twenties achieving really big things. By the end of the sixties, more and more young people were being put in positions of authority and power. There was much more of an expectation then that you would leave college and quite soon you could be doing something really exciting.

I wanted to be the first woman professor of English. When I was first at the grammar school and taking my school work very seriously, I certainly had the idea that the thing to do was to achieve something professionally. As I've said, I got diverted from that somewhat by the kind of group I got in with when I was a bit older, but certainly in my early teens I was clever and wanted to be successful. Even later on when I wasn't working as hard as I should, I still did reasonably well in exams, and there was an assumption that I would go to college, get a degree, and then find a decent job. I definitely didn't want a life like my mother's. I was paranoid about the idea of getting pregnant young. I thought that these men, like my father, stepfather and grandfather, had completely screwed up her life. I was very resentful about the way she had been forced to leave school. She had wanted to do a maths degree, but her father made her leave school and get a job. Then she got pregnant and had to get married, and was eventually left by my father and so forth. I was very militant about not wanting my life to be ruled by babies and men – but I think at that time it wasn't unusual to think like that.

I was very aware of how important money was to independence. In fact, I was very aware of money generally, because we just didn't have any. Most of my friends were more comfortably off than we were. We were always scraping by. We never had any decent furniture. We rarely bought new clothes. My mother bought lots of things from Oxfam and places like that, and occasionally made clothes. However, I really didn't have any high expectations. I hoped that I would be better off than my mother, but I never thought I was going to have lots of money. I was brought up not to be very materialistic, with maxims like 'people come round to see you, not the furniture', and generally to think that what you were doing and the people you knew were more important than having lots of money and being very comfortable. I don't know if I particularly wanted a higher standard of living than my mother's. I think I just wanted more control over what I was doing than I felt my mother had had, and to do that I knew I would need some sort of financial independence.

It's funny – I never really doubted that I would get a job and that I could get a good one and so forth, but I can also remember thinking that it would be wonderful just to drop out and spend my time walking around the Downs in my long skirt and no shoes. I admired people like Janis Joplin, Hendrix and so forth, and thought that it would be wonderful to be somewhere like Monterey and go to pop festivals and not be tied into school or the working world. I wish I had been old enough to go and see the Stones in Hyde Park in 1969, but I was a bit young then for all that. It must have been the beginning of the seventies before I came up to London to hear Frank Zappa and the Mothers of Invention and for David Bowie's first tour.

I didn't come up to London all that much in my early teens, though I can remember coming up once with my brothers to see David. He had a flat in Kensington at the time and we went to Biba where I bought the yellow and purple lipsticks I mentioned earlier. I'd been really keen to go to Biba. I'd heard so much about it and my mother had got some things from there by post, like this incredible purple towelling bikini that floated off you every time that you went near the water. It was a really ugly garment, but Biba did seem to symbolise a lot of things I thought I wanted then. We went to Carnaby Street too on that trip, but it didn't have the glamour of somewhere like Biba. It was already starting to become a bit passé. Soon after that I started thinking that I would like to live in London or perhaps Paris. I was attracted to the idea of capital cities.

I don't think I had great ambitions to travel, but I did want to go to glamorous places. Anyway, we didn't have the money for travel. I went to France on an exchange right at the end of the sixties, but before that the only holidays we had were going to visit either relatives or friends around the country. I used to go off on the train by myself to visit my grandmother who lived in Bolton. We never went abroad, although I had friends who did. One girl I knew used to go off around Europe every summer with her family in a sort of camper van. They'd go to France and Italy and Germany. Her father was a lecturer at the polytechnic. Another friend was half-Danish and used to go off to Denmark on holiday. But most of the people I was at school with had never been abroad, and going on exchanges was often the first time they went outside England. My mother didn't go abroad until she went to Paris for a holiday when she was engaged at about the age of 20. Then the next time she went abroad was when she came to visit me when I was living in Paris when I was 18. People in Bristol would go off to Pembrokeshire for beach holidays, or they would go off to Devon or Cornwall. They'd hire a caravan or a cottage or they'd go camping or visiting relatives. Package holidays were coming in, but hadn't really taken off yet. Until the late sixties, I think it was still quite unusual, certainly for families, to fly off on holiday, but people had quite different expectations then.

So apart from thinking occasionally what it would be like to live somewhere like trendy London and be part of all that scene, I was quite happy with our life in Bristol. I didn't feel any need to break away from my background or rebel against the way my mother brought me up. She kept me on a very, very long leash. I was given a lot more freedom than most of my friends. Some of them were quite envious of me, although sometimes, as I've said, I'd wish that we had a more normal home life. However, like most young teenagers, I was mainly caught up with my own personal emotions at the time. I was quite a daydreamer. I would daydream about being Greta Garbo. I had quite a lot of heroines. I was a very self-contained young person. I still spent a lot of my time reading and I can remember being quite solitary. I often felt rather detached from what was going on around me, which is odd considering that there were always people hanging around our house. Someone would come to a party and end up moving in for three months, because they had been chucked out of their lodgings or had split up with their boyfriend or husband. Then there were the drama students and actors from the Old Vic who lodged with us at various times, and of course the boys from the poetry circle. There would nearly always be a group sat round the kitchen table. It was a very open and warm environment to grow up in.

Because of the drama students and actors, we used to see quite a lot of shows at the Old Vic. Also, my mother had always been very keen on the theatre and, although we didn't have much money then, that was something that was made quite a priority. I can remember seeing Brecht and quite a lot of Shakespeare and also modern stuff, like Albee and Miller's *The Crucible*. I liked Shakespeare, but I think I preferred the modern stuff. I was really interested in theatre and I had phases of wanting to be an actress or wanting to work in the theatre. I got to see stuff through school as well. We were taken on a trip to see *Oh, What a Lovely War*, and also to Stratford. These were whole day trips. They were wonderful, just bliss. I don't remember coming up to see anything in London until the early seventies, and even then I missed the really big events like Brook's *Midsummer Night's Dream*. I'd heard about things like *Hair*, but I don't think I was particularly sold on the idea. I thought I would be embarrassed if I saw people naked on the stage, and by the time I was of an age to go and see something like that, it had been going on for ages and was all a bit old hat anyway.

I also went to the cinema a lot. My mother was a member of the Bristol Arts Centre and we saw some really good films there. I can remember seeing *Rosemary's Baby*, and I think later on that film with Mick Jagger in it – *Performance*. Then we got a television and I watched quite a lot of that too. We'd had a television when we were living with David, but when we moved out we didn't have one for a long time. We couldn't afford it, but eventually we were given one. There was this strange bloke who was the brother of a friend of mine and he was a real maverick. He was much older, in his early thirties, and he'd worked with the Rolling Stones and other groups on tour. He wore these extraordinary skin-tight velvet flares – you know, skin-tight at the top and flared at the bottom. He was a bit of hippy and he'd been involved with drugs. Anyway, he came to see us once and brought us this television, which someone had given him. He also left us all these records, because he had this whole idealistic thing about books and records having to be recycled. He would borrow books from people and then recycle them to other people and things like that. It was very odd, but he was a fairly mad person. I later went out with him, for my sins.

Television had been quite strictly regulated when we'd first had one when I was younger. We were allowed to watch things like *Blue Peter*, but we could never stay up late to see anything. It wasn't until I started babysitting in my early teens that I saw late-night stuff. I used to hope that I would have to babysit when something like *Rowan and Martin's Laugh-In* was on, so I could stay up and watch it. That programme made a big impact on me. I liked comedy shows. I vaguely remember *Monty Python* starting. That was right at the end of the sixties, I think. I also liked watching *The Avengers* and *Z Cars*, which was quite exciting at the time, especially after *Dixon of Dock Green*. It was like a completely new generation of police series.

Television made me more aware of things outside the home. I was aware of things like the Vietnam War going on, although I didn't really understand a great deal about it. And, as I mentioned earlier, I remember the Kennedy assassination. There I was sitting on the floor watching *Blue Peter* and there was this newsflash that President Kennedy has been assassinated, flashing every few minutes on the screen. It was very dramatic. It shocked me deeply. I think it was the first time that anything outside the home really made a big impact on me. Of course, it was reported in such a sensationalist way, but people getting assassinated seemed to be much rarer then. There was much less of that kind of thing about. The world seemed more settled. But suddenly this incredibly important person was killed. There was such a big general feeling that Kennedy was a good thing. He and Jackie were sort of idolised. To many people it was like here was this young couple in the States, who seemed to be changing the world in some way.

However, the Kennedy assassination is the only big political event of the sixties that I have any strong memory of. I don't think I can remember any other political events. My mother and stepfather had the odd political argument, but I don't remember there being really that much talk about politics in our house, which is funny because I always think of my mother as having been very politically committed. In a way she was, but I don't think she was very actively involved until later on. She really didn't have time when the boys were young. She was more into general socialising and trying to make friends. I've got an idea that she joined CND at some point, but I don't think she went on marches. Though at one stage we did have this woman staying with us who did. She was very active and wore a duffle coat and all the rest of the 'uniform' the CND lot used to wear.

I was aware of issues like race and class. We would never buy anything from South Africa and I knew about the Germans in the war and anti-Semitism. But none of it seemed all that relevant to my life. I'd been brought up in very white, small English towns. Even in Bristol when I was 11, I can only remember knowing a few black people. There were a couple of black boys in my class, but I just took them for granted. The Civil Rights Movement in the States was mentioned at school and I remember posters of Martin Luther King, but it all seemed very theoretical. I knew that what was going on in South Africa or America was terrible, but none of it seemed to apply to these black boys in our class.

The only political thing I ever did in my teens was to join the Bristol Union of School Students. That may have been later in the early seventies, but it was the kind of thing that grew out of sixties thinking. We would sit around and discuss student power and how we were going to revolutionise our school, how we were going to change the curriculum, and all that sort of stuff. I also remember talking about the schoolkids' edition of *Oz*. I can remember seeing one, but I don't think it was mine. I did have a copy of *The Little Red Schoolbook* though. None of my friends were allowed to buy a copy, but I had one and we'd read through the bits about sex and contraception and things like that.

Really I wasn't very interested in politics. I didn't realise how hard all the new freedoms had been fought for, that they'd come out of political action. But I was aware of how much things had changed, because of the way my life had changed, and I felt strongly about women's equality and the importance of society being fairer. I can't imagine what it would have been like growing up at any other time. The only thing I sometimes think is that it would have been nice to have been a little bit older, and therefore more able to have been involved in some of the things that were going on. But I was mature for my age and I was affected by what my mother and her friends were doing. The social changes created in the sixties dictated to a certain extent what happened to my family. Ten or even five years earlier, my mother probably wouldn't have behaved as she did and I would have grown up with quite different attitudes. If I'd been born five years earlier or if my mother had left my father five years later, my childhood would have felt much more traditional. I think the underlying liberalisation, the sense of expansion and that things were possible, and the Labour government, all those things actually created a new social climate that shaped the attitudes of the people around me. Certainly it's very unlikely that the sort of household I grew up in could have existed before the sixties.

ELIZABETH

I was born in West Africa, but my parents had great faith in the British education system, so they sent their children to schools in England. When the sixties started, I was at boarding school in Sussex. It was a very international, unEnglish school. There were kids there from all over the world – my friends were from Hong Kong or Persia or wherever – though I think at the time my sister and I arrived there, which was in the mid-fifties, we probably were the only black girls there. By the time we left there were quite a few from Africa, from places like Nigeria and Ghana, and a few from the West Indies. But even at the beginning we never felt particularly out of place or disadvantaged at all. Though, I must admit we were already aware of being treated differently by some people. In fact, I was aware of that from the moment I stepped foot in this country. It ranged from sheer curiosity to all the questions about how do you know when you are dirty, or does it come off, and can I touch your hair and all that, which you just have to get used to, get annoyed by or whatever. Also I remember when my parents were looking for a school, there was one school in particular where the headmistress said, 'I don't mind, but the parents of the other girls ...' So with that sort of thing going on, we were aware in a way of the possibility of prejudice. But it didn't worry me. I mean it was just one of those things and having got into a school, I can't remember every being treated very differently there because I was black. As I've said, at the schools I went to there were lots of kids from all parts of the world, so I just felt normal I suppose.

What was more of a problem was trying to be happy at boarding school as I became a teenager. I was academically very precocious. By the age of 15 I'd done a year in the sixth form and I was fed up with being at boarding school. And there I was, because of the university entrance age, faced with the prospect of having to stay on at school till I was 18! All my friends, who were older, were leaving to go off and do other things and I didn't want to be left behind, so I left too and did A-levels by myself. I did spend some time at a college in London, where various school friends of mine already were, preparing for university entrance, Oxbridge and that kind of thing. I think I'd already got a university place by then but had to wait another year before I was old enough to take it up. I met my future husband during that year.

Anyway, I eventually went to London University to do history. I never questioned the idea of going to university. I just did it because I thought it was what one did after school. I think it was assumed that you tried to get into university after your A-levels and you did whatever subject you were best at. Your choice of subject had absolutely nothing to do with what your future career was going to be or anything else.

London University wasn't like being on a university campus. I never even lived in the college halls of residence, so in a way going to lectures was just like going to work everyday. Often I didn't feel I was at university at all. I was just living in London and doing whatever I was doing. In fact, I'm not sure I learned very much at university that I wouldn't have learned in three years of reading or doing anything else. I don't think I was really into my course. All I remember is thinking that most of it was fairly irrelevant. And I also remember thinking that I had gone through the whole of my education without actually having learned anything about black history or culture. Practically nothing in my university course even mentioned black people. It was only when I did a special option in American history towards the end, that I actually came across things that had something to do with black people, and then only to do with black Americans in this century.

I know I always felt that there was a definite gap. Even at school, I can remember reading newspapers and cutting things out and collecting various articles that I suppose were to do with subjects like African independence and things happening in the States, like the Civil Rights Movement and so on. That was probably all to do with supplementing the diet of the education system, which didn't really touch on the African subjects which I was personally interested in.

When I was at university – certainly in my year – there weren't any other black people in my college. I was the only black person there, so there wasn't anyone to band together with. There was just me and all the other people. Funnily enough, a couple of years ago I met a black woman who had also been at my college but later. She must have come the year after I left and she said she had always wanted to meet me because everybody had always called her by my name. They had just got used to there being one black woman around. I'd left and she'd come along and they'd assumed it was still me!

Up until I left university, I really had very little contact with other black people while I was in this country. It was obviously different when I was in Africa, but it was only when I was in London after university that I became part of the black community here, if you like. When I was at school in Sussex and at university, I came across so few black people, that there was no sense at all of being part of a community as such. I can remember, for example, when I was at school I used to spend holidays with an English family in Sussex. I can remember once meeting some young black guy who had been adopted by a white family and this to me was quite a moment. There was some other black child in the area! That was how much of an outsider one felt. You know, you were always on the outside, you were always an exception, you were always standing out in some way, whether or not you were trying to conform or fit in. I mean, you couldn't conform. You were 'the black kid' or 'the black girl' or the 'black' whatever. It's quite bizarre being forced into a situation where you have to accept being considered exotic.

There was no way I could have conformed to anything in this country. There was no point even trying, and I probably wouldn't have wanted to. I couldn't have done. I know there are a lot of black people who think their ambition is to blend into their surroundings, to be really good and unobtrusive and then everybody will like them, but it can never happen. In the end, you are just who you are. People either like you or they don't like you. You're either good or not good at whatever it is you are doing. You are just who you are. That's true for anybody, and unless you want to spend your life being extremely unhappy you must accept that and just be yourself. I mean if I wanted to become a politician or Prime Minister, I could only do it from where I am and who I am and what I believe. You can only change things by what you do. You can choose what you do only with who you are. That is, I suppose, what I've come to believe. Though, of course, my family background has played a huge part in allowing me to think like that.

My parents were always ambitious for their children and insistent that they gave us a good education. We have never thought of ourselves as disadvantaged or that something was impossible for us because we are black. I'm sure my parents hoped that I would go back home to Africa after university, so I was brought up to expect that I would probably have a comfortable professional life in a country where I wasn't seen as exotic or different or where people might be prejudiced against me because of my colour. I'm sure part of my attitude comes from having been brought up with those sort of expectations, and, actually, apart from the odd thing, my life here has really been like that. Though I still don't feel British, even after having spent more time here than I did in Africa. That doesn't mean that I don't relate to things over here.

One thing I had to contend with in this country, as far as discrimination is concerned, was the problem of finding somewhere to live. I had all the hassles that black people usually have. The first time I had to deal with this was when I came to London, though it wasn't the first time I had encountered prejudice. But finding accommodation of my own was the first time I had to deal with prejudice in a practical way by myself. I know it's difficult for anyone finding accommodation in London, unless of course you've got lots of money. I knew white students who were also having problems, but obviously they didn't have to put up with being told things like 'no coloureds' and 'I don't mind. It's the other people!'

While I was at university, I lived in all sorts of places. I went through all sorts of living situations. I lived in the YWCA for a night or two and I shared a flat briefly with someone from school, but that was only available for a short time. Sometimes I'd end up staying with my boyfriend, not just because I wanted to but because I didn't have anywhere else to go. I even stayed in private hotels. I can remember there were a few weeks when I only had about £10 a week to live on, and I had to spend £8 of that on the hotel. I remember having to work out that I could either take a bus to college, or wherever I was going, or I could have a sardine sandwich for lunch, but I couldn't do both. Then eventually I got into a hostel, sharing a room with a friend.

But apart from the accommodation thing, I enjoyed my time in London at university. I was getting involved with lots of arty, cultural things I suppose – cinema and theatre, poetry and stuff like that. I don't really remember any particular events. The Beatles were taking off then. I liked The Beatles, but I suppose the music I was really into in a big way was jazz and soul. I can remember going to a lot of jazz venues and places like that. I think I was much more aware of American culture. There was more that I related to happening in America, though I didn't actually visit America during the sixties.

Mainly I just got on with my course and was involved in what you might call 'serious' cultural activities. I definitely wasn't involved in the 'swinging London' of 'sex 'n' drugs 'n' rock 'n' roll'. But one way I do remember the new youth culture really affecting me was to do with clothes. What defines the sixties for me in terms of clothes is, from never being able to find anything to fit me, suddenly I could. I'm only 5′ 2″ and very slightly built. In the first half of the sixties, and before that, they didn't seem to make much at any size below size 12, so I was having to make all my own clothes. I could never buy anything that fitted me in the first half of the sixties, but in the second half I could. I think I actually went through a phase of being very clothes-conscious, which must have been to do with so much being suddenly available. Also there weren't really 'teenagers' before the sixties. There were just kids and grown-ups, and I suppose part of my becoming so clothes-conscious at that time was because it coincided with a lot of things suddenly being made available specifically for my age group. I remember Carnaby Street and shopping in Biba and all that. I bought clothes there. There they were, all these wonderful clothes suddenly available in size 8 and 10. I must have bought my first mini-skirt while I was at university, some time around 1965. I've probably still got some of those clothes.

I didn't feel I was doing anything daring or rebellious wearing these short, skimpy clothes. I wasn't trying to shock. They were just what one wore. And, remember, I was already at university by this time, away from home, away from my parents, so I didn't have any older authority figure to rebel against, no parents saying 'You can't wear that' or 'Don't do that'. Anyway I was already different. Being black, I was already an outsider. I was different from most people in my situation, I was different from everything. I didn't have any choice. I mean, who was my role model? Whatever was available, I alone decided what I was going to do, then I did it.

But the big thing I remember from then was not the clothes or the music or anything like that. It was a feeling of anything being possible. Anything was possible no matter what your background, particularly if you were young. My parents obviously thought differently. When they were young it was different and there was some pressure on me to become a professional. They wanted me to be a doctor or a lawyer. Most of my family seem to be doctors and lawyers. It probably took my parents by surprise that I didn't end up being either.

After university, I applied for all sorts of arts and media

jobs and usually got interviews and often job offers, though that was another area where I would sometimes have to deal with prejudice in a practical way. You'd see a job advertised, you'd phone up and arrange an interview and your name didn't sound foreign and your voice didn't sound foreign, but you'd turn up and suddenly everything changed. Maybe that's why after my first few jobs I started the agency. I actually started up my *own* company.

I don't think anyone thought I would survive longer than a year. People were fairly patronising. In fact, I always maintain that a lot of people who started up similar companies afterwards must have thought, 'If a young twit like her can do it, why can't I?' But I never thought a great deal about the difficulties and hassles involved. I just got on with it. I just worked very hard. It never seemed like some terrifying risk that I was taking, giving up the security of a job and plunging into all this. I think I was just so young and idealistic and didn't really know what was involved in setting up a business. Anyway I didn't have great financial commitments at the time – no mortgage or anything like that.

I wouldn't find it so easy today to do something like that. For a start, it's a bloody tiring thing to do. You need an awful lot of energy. It was really gruelling, working in the office at midnight and so on. But I also felt much more in control at that age than I do now, much more confident, much more able to go into unknown situations. Maybe it was a combination of being a certain age at a certain time, like at the end of sixties when anything seemed possible – especially if you were young. Maybe it was to do with the emerging youth culture then, when there were lots of young people doing things, being enterprising in one way or another. Though I still think somebody who's twenty years younger than me could do it now, but in a different sort of way. I think it really is mainly to do with age, because one of the things about starting anything when you are very young is this sense of urgency, the need to get on with things and experience things *now.* When you are in your twenties or in your teens, 30 seems such a long way off. I can remember thinking, 'Oh God, by the age of 30 I'll be dead or I'll have done everything!' You've simply got to get on with things because that's where it all ends, after 30.

About a year after I started the business, I got married. It was a fairly typical register-office-type wedding – not a very romantic do! I seem to remember it being quite casual. My mother and sister were there, and there was his mother and sister and a cousin or two of mine. It wasn't any big deal. We didn't even have a proper honeymoon, just a weekend with a couple of friends of mine who had this cottage on the south coast. Getting married was just a formality one went through. I think I just saw it as something that one did and got out of the way and then got on with one's life as usual.

If my family were disappointed that I didn't have a traditional white church wedding, they didn't show any sign of it, though they were probably totally disappointed in me for all sorts of reasons, which they didn't pass on. I think they were probably more concerned that I was getting married to some sort of musician, even though he came from a very respectable background. They probably had qualms about me not being supported or having a stable lifestyle, but they certainly didn't voice them. I think I just said, 'Listen, I'm getting married,' and that was it. They probably didn't have much say in how it was done. Besides, neither my husband nor I had any particularly strong religious beliefs.

I can't even remember the specific decision to get married. It just seemed a progression. We'd been around together for a long time. There wasn't a point at which we said, 'Let's get married.' It just seemed to happen – just as though it had been assumed. You see, at the beginning of the sixties, and well into the sixties in fact, it was just accepted that if you went out with someone for a long time and you got on, then you'd get married. I suppose there was this accepted progression of things that happened in one's life, just like you'd go through school, then perhaps on to university and so on. It wasn't really until the end of the sixties that things like the Pill were starting to change things, that all these ideas of sexual liberation and freedom and not being committed became fashionable. The sixties really spanned two very different attitudes.

For me, it never felt odd being committed to one person. I never felt constricted or tied down. We were doing things and having a good time together. I can't specifically remember feeling I was missing out on anything. I can't even remember what was happening in London at the time – maybe it just passed me by. I suppose basically how much you were affected by all the new ideas, about sex and society and all that, depended upon whether you already had an ongoing relationship or whether you were just sort of fancy-free and able to enjoy looking for whatever it was you thought you were looking for. I thought I had found what I was looking for.

It wasn't a very conventional marriage, partly I suppose because he was a musician. I've forgotten what happened. In the beginning, when we were first married, I was working and he wasn't and there were periods when I was subsidising him. I was earning for us both. Quite often, as a musician, he wouldn't get much work for months at a time and sometimes he would go off on tour, so he wouldn't be around anyway. Sometimes he'd take on any old job, which meant a steady income for a while. But it wasn't really a typical, conventional sort of marriage and it eventually broke up. I don't know if that was to do with what we were doing. I think it was really to do with the fact that we'd got together so young, just grew into different people and grew apart.

I think it was a fairly equal relationship. As I said, there were points when I was providing for us both and I'm sure he did as much cooking and cleaning as I did. I think it was an odd mixture of me working, sometimes supporting us both and having my own life, and also taking on board various conventions that I probably assumed I should conform to. For instance, I can remember when he had this really boring office job somewhere in south London.

We were living in Islington at the time and he had to get up really early to get to wherever this company was, and I started getting up first to prepare a packed lunch for him. At one point I used to knit jumpers for him and I hate knitting! Maybe I did these things out of a feeling I had that that was what a good wife ought to do, though I don't remember anybody ever telling me that was the case, neither my husband nor any of my family. I think it was just me. I obviously went through a phase of thinking, 'Well, maybe, this is what I should be doing. At least try and conform to some notion of what a good woman should do to support her man.' That didn't last very long!

I certainly didn't see marriage in terms of 'settling down', however. I don't think I ever thought I was going to stay at home and have a child and all the rest of it, because I was already involved with a career of my own. It definitely wasn't conventional 'settling down', even though it may have been conventional getting married in the first place. I'd already decided that I was going to have my own company and my own career. I was never brought up to think that girls got married and just 'settled down' and that was it. I was brought up to think that having a profession was a definite possibility and so there wasn't any great internal revolution to get to that point. It was something that had always been a possibility and it just came about. I suppose my rebellion was starting something like the agency, which had no precedent in the circles I came from, not the fact that I had a career or didn't confirm to some sort of traditional image of a married woman.

My husband was very encouraging about my business. In fact, he was always like that about most things I got involved with. In many people's eyes I must have seemed more successful than him, but that didn't seem to bother him either. Though, thinking back, maybe it did. Maybe he wasn't happy with such an equal relationship. Maybe it contributed to the break-up of the marriage, but who knows? We still see each other and we're still friendly.

It's very strange thinking back about my marriage and other things. I think I was just so much of a freak anyway in most circles that I didn't conform to anything. I don't remember going through all the sort of liberating feelings of the sixties that a lot of other people seem to have experienced. I was probably just different anyway. I simply felt I had a right to do things no matter what the conventions were and that was that. I feel I would have been like that whether it was the sixties or the fifties or whenever. I already felt I was different, an outsider. In fact, far from *consciously* wanting to be 'liberated' and 'do my own thing', perhaps I even felt some mild pressure to conform. Perhaps I wanted to be like everybody else in some ways, which was what the trying to be a good wife and making the sandwiches and all that kind of thing was about.

Certainly, for much of my growing up, I was made to feel different from everybody else. As I've said, there simply weren't lots of black people around. I was the only black person here or the only black women there. The other day, I came across a press cutting from when I started the agency. All the publicity I got was sort of freakish. It all centred on me, because I was black and because I was a woman. The whole thing was very strange. I was being a regarded as a freak, which I suppose I was in a way. I mean there weren't many women, let alone black women, doing the kind of thing I was doing ... and there still aren't.

I'm not saying that I actually saw myself as non-conformist. I was just *me*. I was just being myself. And, as I've said, I never consciously felt part of the youth movement of the sixties. I was surrounded by all this stuff going on in London at the time, all the boutiques and fashions and the King's Road and that kind of thing, but I don't remember thinking any of it was especially glamorous or that it was something that I *had* to be a part of. It may have seemed to some people that I was really involved in all that, because I was doing something creative and running my own business. But it just happened that I was a certain age then, 18 and 19, or 20 or 22, a time when I would be starting up and becoming independent anyway. I suppose I was just being me, doing what I wanted, at a time when it was starting to become the fashionable thing to be like that.

Of course I wasn't totally disinterested in what was going on in the London social scene at the time. I've already said that I was fairly interested in clothes for a while, but that was largely because I could suddenly find things to fit me. And I had this huge Afro. Before that I had had my hair straightened. On my wedding photograph, my hair is straight. I look like one of The Supremes, but so many black women did then. The whole thing about what black people do to their hair goes back generations. It's got to do with trying to be accepted, assimilating with white culture. That's why the whole Civil Rights Movement in America in the sixties was so liberating. It helped start the 'Black is Beautiful' thing, which had a tremendous influence on the way black youngsters or teenagers saw themselves in the sixties. Suddenly you were proud to be black, and you could wear your hair natural! That was the real fashion landmark of the sixties for me. It wasn't whether one's skirt was a certain length or not.

Being a musician's wife, I mixed a lot in the London jazz scene. Smoking joints was very much part of the jazz scene, but I can't remember anybody being into really hard drugs – heroin or anything like that. I never really got involved with drugs. I never tried LSD. I think I was probably a bit wary of it, having heard stories of people who had had bad trips and things. And I certainly never felt I was missing anything.

I never thought of myself as mixing with the 'right' kind of people or being part of a particular scene. Maybe some of the people I saw around the jazz clubs felt like that. A lot of them had the spectre of working in a bank, in say Bromley West, and coming to the clubs was their way of escaping, of rebelling against the respectability and boredom of their daily lives. But I didn't feel I was being rebellious, going to these clubs and things. It didn't seem likely that I'd ever be working in a bank, so I didn't feel that I had anything to rebel against. Though I suppose in a way I had rebelled. What I might have ended up doing, if I had not done what I was doing, is going back to Africa and just being a professional. That was what was plotted out for me by my parents.

But even not fitting in with my parents' plans wasn't conscious rebellion. I had always wanted to do something in the arts and the agency really grew out of that. I think it was obvious from quite early on that I might do something a little away from the norm. I didn't think I was taking a great risk in doing something like that or that it might be insecure. Young people didn't worry so much about money and job security then. I got my first mortgage only about three years ago. That is a very definite difference between then and now. It was cheap then to live in London. I suppose as well there were certain assumptions that every-body had about life then. For example, you could always get a job and there was never any question of not being able to change your job if it didn't work out. I was able to leave a job and risk starting a business. I wasn't earning a lot of money, but I didn't need to and that wasn't anybody's business but mine.

When I started the agency, I didn't think in terms of having a turnover of so and so by a certain date. Nothing was that planned. I suppose my ambition was to support and encourage projects that more conventional organi-sations wouldn't handle. I'm sure I might have thought, 'I'm going to be a millionaire by the time I'm 25 or some-thing,' but it wasn't worked out with that aim. You could say that my motives were idealistic. I'm sure people starting a business now would have to do it on a much more business-like basis. But the late sixties were very idealistic. It was part of that thing of feeling that anything was possible or that things seemed to be more possible for young people and you could start up a business on 2/6! Though not everybody started a business, so I suppose what I did was a combination of that idealism and having the sort of personality that made me not mind taking risks.

Starting something like a business then was more an attitude of 'doing your thing' rather than 'I am starting a business'. I didn't do a lot of financial planning. If I'd been mainly looking to make a large profit, I wouldn't have gone into something like the agency in the first place! I think people now just seem to be more realistic about life in terms of finance and all the rest of it than it ever seemed necessary to be in the sixties. Actually I don't think it would have made that much difference to me if I had looked at the financial side more. It might have made some difference later on, but I don't think the starting up was really linked that much to business knowledge. In fact, I suspect that it might have worked the other way round. If I'd really sat down and analysed what I was proposing to do in a business-like way, it might not have seemed at all sensible in the first place. I might have ended up being put off completely. Though I'm not trying to suggest that the attitude towards business in the sixties was any better than now – I'm sure there were as many disasters as there were successes – it's just that I think it was easier then to take a risk.

Looking back at the sixties, I'm never sure whether things generally were better or easier to do then than now. I certainly can remember all sorts of high feelings, feelings of everything being really good and enjoying the music and the company I mixed in and what I was doing. But I don't know if that was the sixties or just to do with the age I was then. Really I think that there is a stage in your life when you have lots of ideas about the way you want your life to go, whether its to do with your career or waiting for the love of your life to show up or whatever. It's a time when there always seems to be the prospect of something good being just about to happen or everything is waiting for you. Whether that time occurs for you in the sixties – or fifties or seventies or eighties – there must be such a period in your life. You could call it 'a golden era'.

However, maybe I took too much for granted. Maybe it wasn't just my age that made me feel the way I did then and it really was something to do with the spirit of times that made me feel so high about everything. Perhaps the sixties was in fact a very special period, aside from what I happened to be doing. I mean if you look at all the stuff that's been said and written about the sixties, it obviously was an extraordinary time. I suppose it is just hard for me to disassociate what I was doing and who I was then from what was going on generally. I wonder what it would have been like ten years later, if I had been trying to do the same kind of things that I was doing then. Would I have felt the same? Maybe not. Actually, another strange feeling is that I am much more aware of the sixties and of the eighties than of the seventies. The seventies were a sort of non-era, a hiatus. I'm left with a feeling that nothing much was happening then. There was no particular aroma of the decade in the seventies like there was in the sixties. It was as though it was just a continuation or an extension of what was happening in the sixties. There was definitely an excitement, a feeling of possibility in the air in the late sixties, that was independent of the way I felt.

Talking like this, has made me think a lot more about what was happening then. I think to be honest, it actually was a period of great possibility, perhaps a sort of golden age that may never come again. Because it was all happening then, because it all seemed so possible then. Maybe one assumed that it would always be possible and perhaps that's why there is a certain feeling of let-down for many people now. Maybe it was a good thing that the sixties coincided with the period in my life when I was starting out and there was so much I wanted to do. I think I am often too blasé about it all and take too much for granted. Perhaps I should just say, 'Gosh, it was lucky that I happened to be the age I was then and wanted to do certain things when it was much more possible just to go ahead and do them.'

But also, as I've said before, I think there was a definite break between the first half of the sixties and the second half of the sixties. I'm sure there was an actual break in terms of the access there was to certain things, different sorts of literature or people or whatever . . . and there was also a break in attitudes and expectations. Things didn't really start to change and open up until the second half of the sixties, though I suppose even then it probably affected me more being in London and mixing in academic and media circles. I suspect that had I got married just a few years earlier, at the beginning of the sixties, a lot of things in my life might have been different. I would probably have felt then that when you got married, you ought to have kids.

I certainly know a lot of people who are just a few years older than me and who come from a similar sort of background, but they have two or three kids who are now in their twenties. They just got married in the late fifties or early sixties and did what was expected. They had their kids. I suspect that if I had got married in the first half of the sixties, I would have fitted into that pattern too. As it was, attitudes were starting to change by the time I got married, so I felt it was all right to have a career and not have kids. The Pill was there by then too. You didn't have to get pregnant instantly. I suppose if the Pill hadn't been around I probably would have had several kids by the end of the sixties!

Actually, if I'm honest, I don't think I ever wanted to have children and the Pill and changes in attitude just made it easier for me not to. Mostly, people actually only do what they really want to do or they just conform to their background and the expectations of their families, whether it's in the sixties or the seventies or the eighties. I think I saw myself as very independent, but even I must have been tied to certain traditions and expectations. Perhaps if I'd been a couple of years younger, I wouldn't have got married at all. Maybe I was just in the middle, not quite old enough to be completely conventional but not quite young enough to sort of do away with it all. Now I think about it, that was exactly what must have happened, because I can't really think of any other reason why I chose to go through the motion of getting married and sometimes pretending to be a housewife. I think perhaps I was actually straddling that change from being totally conventional and being totally unconventional.

Obviously some sort of residual feeling that one ought to get married, rather than just live with someone, made me get married, but there wasn't enough of that feeling to say one ought to have 2.3 children in the next few years. So I accepted a bit and discarded a bit.

In fact, we did sort of live together for a while, but not officially and not wholly. I shared a flat with my sister and he shared a flat with another friend and we sort of stayed over most of the time at each other's places. But we didn't formally set up house together until we were married. So that was maybe another dividing point, when people did start thinking it was okay just to live together. I think it probably wouldn't have been quite proper to do it in the first half of the sixties. It probably all changed in 1967 when we got married! You know, I think that may well be it, that a year or two either side and my whole life would have been completely different. Strange to think of it that way. What a difference a couple of years can make!

SUSAN

I was born in Cardiff and brought up there. I spent my childhood there, and my teens, and didn't really live anywhere else until I came to London at the end of 1969. I was born in 1947, so when I left I must have been 22 or nearly 22 – something like that – and at the beginning of the sixties, I was 13.

Looking back, I realise that Cardiff changed a great deal for me over those years, not just because I was growing up but because my whole world and outlook changed. I'd come from a secure, cosy, comfortable, Jewish middle-class background, rather insular in a way, but when I left I was no longer part of that. I wanted something totally different out of life. I had had the experience of four years in art college and I'd been to America, and that had changed me completely.

Obviously, being Jewish, my parents weren't of Welsh origin. But they were both born in Wales and have lived there all their lives, so in a way they are Welsh. On my father's side, my grandfather had come from Israel. He did the opposite of what a lot of Jews were doing at the time. He came *from* Israel with his young wife and settled in the Valleys. Quite a few Jews settled in the Welsh Valleys. I suppose because they are near the ports and people arriving in the country just moved up from there. My father actually did go back to Israel when he was 11 or 12 taking arms with my grandfather – it was all very exciting. They went through Egypt.

My father came from a very religious family. Actually, my grandparents on both sides of the family were very religious. But by the time I was born, things had already changed a bit. There was still a definite sense of being Jewish. We kept absolutely to kosher food, but my parents didn't go to the synagogue very much, only really on special holidays. I was the one who went to the synagogue regularly. Even at 13, right at the beginning of the sixties, I was still going to the synagogue every week. I was very involved in the social life there – it was quite an important part of my life then. As time went on, I did begin to find it more and more boring, but at 13 I was quite happy to be part of it. I wasn't rebellious. In fact, I didn't really become rebellious until I went to art college when I was 18.

There were quite a lot of Jewish people in Cardiff, but by the early sixties most of them had already moved away from the area we lived in. I went along to the synagogue every Sunday to something called Study Group. And to me, that was very important. It was my whole social life. We would have meetings and would sort of give talks. Then we'd have dancing and singing afterwards. There were two parts of Cardiff – the newer part where most of the Jewish people lived and the older part where I lived with just a few friends – so all of us coming together and meeting up at these Study Groups would be very important to us. We would also have Winter Schools, where we would go away for something like ten days and meet people from all over Britain. These were the things that really kept me involved with religion.

There was a group of Jewish kids at school, about eighteen of us, and we had our own Jewish prayers. We were very aware that we were different and formed a distinct social group, partly because most of us were also meeting up outside school at the Sunday Study Groups. In fact, our conversation at school would revolve around what we were going to do over the weekend at Study Group.

Now, I'm certain that I wouldn't have been as keen on going to the synagogue, if it hadn't been for the fact that my social life was so involved with Jewish kids – I'm sure that's the real reason I went there. I went because my friends did and, like all teenagers, I wanted to belong, not to be an outsider. I didn't have to go. As I've already said, my parents didn't go, except on special holidays, and they certainly didn't insist that I did. I went because lots of my friends did, and occasionally a few of the boys would turn up. That made it very attractive.

I had boyfriends in my teens, but none of them were very serious. It was very much a case of going out with a whole group of people, not just the two of you together. Occasionally, somebody would phone you up and you'd go to a cinema with him, but normally going out was much more of a gang thing. Special relationships tended to form when we went away on courses, like to Winter School. Quite often, the boyfriend was somebody who you would write to and only see every six weeks or so. It was all very adolescent.

There was no real sex involved. The 'sexual revolution' had not yet hit Cardiff, or rather it hadn't hit the closed circle I moved in. I did know girls at school, who at 14 or 15 were already talking about how petrified they were that they might be pregnant. But they were very much in the minority. It's funny, but it was nearly always the girls who weren't particularly interested in school work who seemed to be keen on sex. They were almost like a different class. I think I rather looked down on them – but I was interested in hearing about what they got up to, even if I thought they were being very stupid. The whole thing – the sexual thing and the drugs thing – didn't hit me until much later.

I was interested in clothes, though. I had to wear a school uniform and could only really wear my own clothes at the weekends. But it was important to me that I looked good. I loved going into a shop and buying something that was nice, though I don't think I was really all that aware of fashion until I was about 16. Even then, I think I was still very conventional. It was only later at art school that I can remember shocking people with some of the things I wore. I suppose I then became a bit of a leader of fashion.

I tend to think of fifties fashions as having been rather depressing, especially for men. To me, the fashion revolution of the sixties was a lot about how men's clothing changed, because men and boys had all looked so grey until then and suddenly they were allowed to wear bright colours. I also think the women's underclothing thing was an enormous breakthrough. I remember being told by my mother from a very early age that she wore – well, it wasn't exactly a corset, but this elastic thing that kept your stomach in. There I was wearing that kind of thing when I first began art college. Even then, I must have been an absolute freak wearing that. For me, starting art college was a terrible shock.

The art college environment was the thing that made a lot of difference to me. Really thinking about it, I'm sure that I only really became aware of fashion trends when I went to art college. That was in 1966. It was my complete break with the fifties and my rather conventional background. Maybe a lot of things were going on in London before then, but I wasn't really aware of all the big changes before I went to art college. We would come up to London on day trips to see galleries, and at the same time went into all the various shops around – the Mary Quant place, Carnaby Street, and that place in Kensington Church Street – Biba. We always went to Biba – and to stupid Lawrence Corner. There was a big thing about going to Lawrence Corner at that particular time. It was one of the first places people used to go. Before they went to any gallery, they used to go to Lawrence Corner. I used to go too, looking for all those wonderful things everybody else seemed to get there, only I could never find them. You know, the only interesting thing that ever happened to me at Lawrence Corner is that a woman tried to pick me up.

In my last two years at art school, I kept a diary. That was in 1968 and 1969, when I was 21 and 22. I was looking at this diary recently and every week in my lunch hour I'd been out and bought a new jumper. There was so much in this diary about what I wore when I was at art college. You'd have thought most of the time I would have just worn painted jeans and things, but it was obviously very important to me what I wore there. I felt being an art student gave me a licence to wear exactly what I wanted. I would wear, for example, odd stockings – I remember wearing a turquoise stocking and a mauve stocking. I had to have different colours to go along with my turquoise top and my mauve skirt. All the fashionable colours then were very bright – they really were. My diary mentions one of the lecturers coming in wearing a bright orange shirt and a mauve suit and how he looked so terrific, just brilliant! This was about 1967. God, it was wonderful the way everything had changed!

I can remember wearing mini-skirts when I went to Israel. That was before mini-skirts had ever come out in Israel and they were absolutely astonished. I went to Israel quite a lot. I went to Israel for the first time when I was 17 with a youth group. That was in 1964 – and I went again in 1967, just after the Six Day War. In fact, I think I went in both 1967 and 1968, and maybe even in 1969 as well. I had relatives there that I could stay with and therefore I could easily go there on holiday by myself.

Israel was very important to me at the time. What happened in the Six Day War affected me incredibly. I was listening to the television and the radio all the time. I was really so affected, that I wanted to go over there. I wanted to go over there and volunteer, just to do something to help. I never thought about the danger. And I don't think my parents would have minded me doing that.

Later on, my feelings about Israel came into conflict at college, because it was the time when the whole revolutionary thing was beginning to take place, and it was just starting to become fashionable, right at the end of the sixties, to think that Israel was the aggressor. There were some very anti-Israel remarks made by a few people in college – not directly to me, just generally. But I was really hurt by them, because at the time I was still very bound up with the country. You know, for a while I had thought that I would like to go and live in Israel. It was only art college that changed that. I just didn't think the art in Israel was particularly good, and I couldn't ever imagine myself being able to work well in that sort of society. Otherwise, I would have gone there.

Art college certainly changed a lot in my life. Yet at school, I hadn't had any particular idea about going there. I was a bit aimless and I didn't really know what I wanted to do. I didn't like school particularly. It was only when I got into doing A-levels that I really enjoyed school a lot.

And if it hadn't been for those two years when I enjoyed school so much, I would have actually left Cardiff earlier.

My mother was a medical secretary and she thought it would be nice if I became a medical secretary. She actually wrote away and got me an application form to go to St Godric's to do a medical secretarial course, but then I did very well in my next lot of school exams and I thought, this is crazy, why bother to waste it all and come up to London for that. So instead I stayed on at school and did A-levels. I did history and art. Art was obviously the thing I had more talent in than anything else, but I still had no idea of what I wanted to do. I didn't write away for the application form to go to art college. My mother did. I didn't even want to go for the interview. I just sort of wandered into it, really aimlessly, but when I got there I loved it. Even when I went for the interview I knew I was going to love it.

At that time, it wasn't the life of the college that appealed to me at all. I didn't see going to art college as a trendy thing to do. I was going to learn skills, possibly something to do with fabric design, because that was the way my paintings and drawings were going. However, it ended up completely different from that, because it ended up with me making environments out of hair and kapok and things and having an exhibition at the ICA. It was all very freaky and totally different from anything I had planned or expected.

My nice conventional background hadn't prepared me for anything at art college really. Everything was different to what I'd been used to. I couldn't get over the language. I couldn't believe it when people swore so much. And I think my parents found it difficult. It's funny because they had pushed me into going and afterwards I think they regretted it. In fact, they have pushed me in to several things that they obviously regretted afterwards, because some of those things have changed me so much, making me into the person that I am now, and not the person that they probably wanted me to become.

I think they expected I would just go to college, and

carry on going to Jewish functions where I would meet a nice boy. My having a career really wasn't important. Art college was how I was going to fill in my time before I met that good Jewish man. I have to admit that, before I went to art school, I did fancy being the first person out of our whole crowd of girls to get married. I could see myself walking down the aisle in a wonderful white dress. Then somebody beat me to it and I thought, 'I'm not interested now. It's already been done.' It was just a romantic picture. It didn't have anything to do with reality, with actually getting married.

Most of the girls I grew up with all did exactly what they were supposed to do. They all ended up by getting married in their early twenties or in their late teens. They married solicitors and doctors, usually men in those sorts of jobs. I was the one who got out of it.

Looking back I can see there were two reasons why I broke away. Art college was certainly the main one, but the other was because I had a best friend who was very different from all of the other Jewish girls around. She came from a home where they didn't have a car. Her father was a school teacher and rode a bicycle and they wanted to settle in Israel. Their values were very different from the families of my other friends. She really helped me a lot, I think. I had much more in common with her than with the other girls. She persuaded me to go along to Habonim, which was a socialist organisation. People in Habonim weren't so materialistic and the aim was that eventually you went to live in Israel. So mixing with these people changed my values somewhat, although art college obviously had a bigger effect.

Cardiff Art College was really good at the time. It had been terrible, but had been taken over by a group of lecturers, who had come from somewhere like Leeds or Leicester. They brought a lot of students with them and they transformed the whole place. So I didn't really mind going there and continuing to live at home, although I was quite keen for a change, having spent all my life in Cardiff. In fact, after a year, I did get away.

I went to Hull for what turned out to be just about the most unhappy year of my life. It was just dreadful. I was so unhappy. It was absolutely awful. There was a glue factory there. It stank of fish. And I really knew what total loneliness was. I mean, I just felt I was completely out of place there. It was incredibly dull. Everything reached Hull about five years after it reached everywhere else. It was about 1967 and everywhere else girls were wearing mini-skirts, but in Hull I'm sure they'd never heard of them. And it was so flat. I'd been used to being by the sea and having hills around me. It's funny, but you don't realise how important geography is until you change it. Then you realise how it has actually made you what you are. I just couldn't bear more than a year in Hull, so I came back to Cardiff.

The college then stipulated that if I came back I had to live away from home and that's what I did. I left home and moved into a flat. I was then 19. My parents weren't too keen on my doing that. In fact, they thought it was quite terrible. They couldn't understand why I should want to move out. From their point of view, I had a nice comfortable home with them, so why should I want to live somewhere else. 'What was the point?' they asked.

I shared the flat with a friend, a girl who I had gone to school with and who had moved on to art college with me. She wasn't Jewish, so obviously we weren't keeping a kosher kitchen, but I still didn't eat non-kosher meat. I kept to that, but I'd practically stopped going to the synagogue by now. I did go occasionally, but I was beginning to value my time more and to realise how terrible the services were. I was moving away from a social life that revolved around the synagogue into one that centred on the art college. I'd gone to art college because of the work itself, and that was still the most important thing, but the social scene there was obviously becoming important to me, too. I had a love/hate thing about art college. I hated it in the beginning and found it very hard, but gradually, as whatever talent I had was being recognised by certain lecturers and developed, I found enormous satisfaction in being creative. That became the most important thing in my life. It's hard to express what I felt, but it was really fantastic.

Up to my final year in art college, I did painting. There was a certain snob value put on fine art at Cardiff. You know, that was the thing to do, so although I'd gone in talking about doing fabric design and things, I quickly realised I didn't want to be stuck with a group of women sewing clothes and printing bits of cloth. That became the last thing I wanted. It just didn't seem like much fun. However, I did try it for about three weeks, but I could see what people in the fine art department were up to and I thought that's what I really wanted to do, although it was much tougher. It was also the time when the first art degree courses came out – the DipAD courses – and Cardiff then only had a DipAD for fine art, so anything else that you did was thought of as not being as classy. Also, the people who ran the college, those who had come in and revolutionised the place in the mid-sixties, they were only really interested in the fine art department.

There was a bit of a revolution in art teaching around this time. Everything was really changing and it was very exciting. Cardiff was one of the first places where this happened. I don't think it happened quite as early or as much in London. I was absolutely amazed when I came up to St Martins. I thought that because a college was in London it would be more advanced than Cardiff, but it wasn't. Cardiff was far more advanced. There were only about three or four colleges in Britain as advanced as Cardiff.

I'm not a very precise person. I wouldn't have been interested in a traditional fine art course. When we had a life model, we would look at her in terms of colour or form or texture, not trying to draw her as she was, but trying to express something through her. I did textual painting, using oils. Some of it was put on very thickly, and some would be applied thinly with a sponge or something. Everything I did was involved with texture. For a while I was very involved with doing pictures about cakes. When I was in Hull and very unhappy, the way I got my satisfaction was by eating and I realised I had to transform this into art. So I used to buy a cake and then paint it. I also used to make multi-coloured cakes in weird colours. Actually, later on, when I had one of my exhibitions, I remember having some friends around for supper after the private view and serving bright blue eggs and lots of other strangely coloured stuff – all full of dangerous chemicals, no doubt!

My paintings were semi-abstract rather than figurative. When I painted one of my cakes, you could still tell that it was a cake, but it was done in a particular way, a stylised way. People very rarely used models. You just wouldn't have survived in a place like Cardiff, if you'd painted in a more academic or figurative style. They would never have let you survive. They were very hard, those lecturers. Looking back, I think in some ways they could be so destructive. They thought that they should break everything down, so that something new could come alive. I found it both shattering and exciting. I really had an incredibly tough yet stimulating time.

Our main lecturers usually came down from London. They would do their three- or four-day teaching stint and then go back. They were artists who didn't particularly want to teach, but they had to and they resented it. Some of them were really rather disgusting. They drank a lot and behaved very badly. I remember once one of them peeing into an ashtray in a hotel. At first, I found that kind of behaviour shattering, absolutely shattering. But I realised as time went on that there was no way of completely escaping from being part of all this, because social life revolved around these people.

There was one particular lecturer who had been head of my foundation course. I started off by fearing him, then I began to admire him a lot. He happened to win *the* award of the year at that particular time and somebody like that was hero-worshipped. It was obvious that he fancied me and, whatever else I felt about that, I was flattered. I ended up having an affair with him. It was the first affair I ever had. The whole relationship got very heavy, very involved, and I couldn't escape by pouring myself into my work, because my emotional life and my work were all tangled up together.

When I first went out with him, I wouldn't sleep with him, so he dropped me. Then I found he was leaving. It was like I had nothing to lose. He was going anyway, so I thought it couldn't get too complicated. He was going to go in another two or three months, so I thought I may as well sleep with him because I'm going to lose him anyway. It's a strange way of reasoning, I know, but I'm sure that's what I did think at the time. It's funny, because I was a virgin and, looking back at my diary, I now realise that I lost my virginity on St Valentine's Day 1968. I was 21 – quite old in fact.

He was about 35 and married, though his wife lived away. She lived in London and I'd never seen her. I didn't know anything about her. I knew the relationship wasn't going to materialise into anything, so I didn't feel bad about it. I never thought any of my relationships then would really materialise into anything. I just didn't think like that. It's funny that, even though I'd once had my abstract idea of wanting to get married at a very early age, I never really saw myself actually *being* married. In fact, I think the thing I was afraid of was responsibility. At the time, I never ever wanted responsibility with anything. It's bad enough having responsibility for oneself. Why take on anything else? The thought of actually having to cook meals for somebody – no, I wasn't at all interested in that. The most important thing then was my work. I never thought about having a long lasting relationship with anybody. I just lived for the moment. I never thought about the future. I was often emotionally attached, but I certainly wouldn't have thought about marrying.

My parents were never aware of this change of attitude. By this time I was living away from home and I knew that they would feel better not knowing what was going on. In fact, I never told them about any of my boyfriends. I kept all of that to myself. I couldn't tell them anything like that. They lived in a totally different world. Even now they can still turn round and say, 'Oh, it's terrible that so-and-so is marrying somebody that isn't Jewish.' That's the world that they live in.

I didn't sleep around very much, in fact. It was mainly this one lecturer. After that, I had maybe three or four sort of affairs. You were under so much pressure then to sleep around, so that's what you did. I don't know what it's like now for young people because of the whole AIDS thing, but then there was so much pressure on having to sleep with people. All this sexual permissiveness was supposed to be part of the sixties revolution. A lot of girls seemed to think it was OK. They'd say things like, 'The Pill gives us the freedom to do as we like.' But I'd had such a 'heavy' background that to me it was something that I was never totally happy about. I never really felt it was right to sleep around. Deep down, thinking of the times that I did sleep with people, it was almost because I felt I had to and that really it wasn't what I wanted. I just felt, 'This is what is expected of me, but damn, why is it expected of me?'

I didn't consider going on the Pill. Maybe because the Pill to me meant commitment. It would have meant that I had made a commitment to sleeping around, which, as I've said, wasn't something I really wanted to do. I wasn't a very sexual person. For me it was all more to do with emotion and attraction. It was about the 'high' that came from being admired. But I didn't actually think it was wrong to go on the Pill. I didn't look down on girls who did. At that time, a lot of the people in art college were having serious relationships. Quite a few of the girls I knew were really committed to their boyfriends. I was perhaps one of the few who didn't feel committed to anybody. Also, the Pill for me meant taking drugs, and I didn't like the idea of that then. And another thing, in a place like Cardiff where did you get the Pill from? If you had a sympathetic doctor, it was probably quite easy, but I can't remember there actually being a family planning clinic. In London it might have been a totally different story. Anyway, as it turned out, I was probably stupid not to use the Pill, because I ended up having to have an abortion.

When I first thought I was pregnant, I was petrified, absolutely petrified. The last thing I could do was to tell my parents. And I didn't have any money for an abortion, I didn't have anything. I told the 'father', but he just said that it was nothing to do with him. He said that it was absolutely impossible and that there was no way that it could have been him, and that was that. He certainly wasn't going to help me out as far as any money was concerned. That was it.

A friend gave me the name of a gynaecologist in Harley Street. This was 1968. The law had just been changed and people were coming over to Britain specially to have an abortion. Sometimes, in a strange way, I feel like I played a major part in history, but then all I knew was that I had to go and see this dreadful guy in Harley Street. I had a urine test done in the morning and I had to go back in the afternoon to be told the results. I went into his surgery and he said, 'Yes, well, yes, you're pregnant. Let me show you something.' That particular day an article had come out in *Der Stern* magazine. A lot of German women were coming over at the time and having abortions with him, and there was actually an article about him in this magazine with a picture of him holding a foetus! He actually showed me this picture and said, 'There's me and this foetus that I've just taken out of somebody. Well, what are we going to do about you? It's going to cost you £100.' It was immediately down to business! I was completely shattered.

I still didn't have any money and I didn't know how I was going to get any money. But I remembered that my parents had been collecting money for me in a savings bank since I was little. I managed to get hold of the saving book, went into a post office, and asked to take out £100. At that time, you weren't allowed to take out more than £20 at a time and they refused to do it. I had already been told that unless I actually had the money in cash to take with me to the hospital next morning, there was no way I was going to have an abortion. Then somebody suggested that I went to the main post office, so I did. But the man there still said, 'I'm sorry, but the rules are the rules,' and I started to cry. I said, 'Look, I'm desperate for this money. I really need this money.' The only thing that he could suggest was that I go to a moneylender. I went out crying, then went back in to ask them where the telephone was, so I could get in contact with a moneylender. The women and men were huddled together behind the counter deep in conversation. They saw me, stopped, and said, 'Just give us your book,' and they gave me the money.

So I had my abortion. It was done in St John's Wood, in a very nice clinic, in fact. I didn't feel bad about it. It was only a few weeks since I'd missed my period, so it didn't feel like I was carrying another life. I didn't think I was destroying a life. It didn't mean anything. Morally I felt nothing, but I did feel a physical wreck. I also felt very alone with no one to talk to. I'd had to go through most of this on my own. Except for some support from two women friends, nobody had helped me.

Then when I got back to Cardiff, I was told there was something going around, some minor infection that was supposed to cause women's periods to be late. I began to think that I may not have been pregnant to start off with. Exactly a year later, when I was in America, I was sent an article about this doctor, the one I'd seen in Harley Street. Apparently, it had been discovered that he was telling women they were pregnant when they weren't. Then he would charge them a £100 a time for an 'abortion', which was in fact a simple D and C. It was amazing to see this all written down. I mean, I'd been there and actually gone through all this. I still don't know to this day if I was pregnant or not.

Afterwards I lost a lot of weight. I came back to art school for my last year and just threw myself into my work. It was at that particular time that I started making these environments. I had been gradually moving out of straight painting and more into free-form things – and for a very simple reason: I hated making stretchers! I was very bad at making stretchers. They always seemed to go lop-sided, and so I thought creating environments would be a wonderful way of not having to make stretchers. First of all, I did floor pieces, then the lecturers suggested that perhaps I should think about making them three-dimensional, so the obvious thing was to get this furniture and just cover it. It all grew from there. Before I had time to even finish one piece, I had lots of ideas about what I wanted to do next. I became an absolute workaholic. It was a wonderful year. As far as work was concerned, it was fantastic. I would come in early and work till really late, and I got an enormous amount of fulfilment from it.

I just couldn't work like that now. I've got so many commitments, and yet at the time I felt it was something that I could never give up. I felt that if I stopped I would die. It's a very exhausting thing making environments. I mean, it's exhausting emotionally, because you have to live within a particular environment for a period of time. I found that every time I did it, it was like going through some kind of metamorphosis. You need a lot of space too, and obviously you have to have somewhere to show them. In the economic climate as it is now, that would be really difficult, though even then, in the late sixties and the start of the seventies, the money was beginning to run out. When I was at college, I couldn't do a total environment. I would do, say, a couple of chairs and floor piece or a bookcase or something like that. Only when I came to London and had two or three exhibitions, was I able to do a whole environment. If I had gone to America it might have been different. I could have done much better there. They seemed to have the money and space.

I did go to America, in fact, but only on a visit, just after I finished at art school. I had a friend who I had met the year before in Israel. She lived in New York and she persuaded me to go over, so I went for two months. She lived in the Bronx, a really Jewish area. Her family had lived there for years and years. I thought it was horrible, absolutely awful. I was quite frightened travelling back there on the subway. I can remember once catching the wrong train and ending up in a black ghetto and being quite scared by all of it. Remember, I had come from Cardiff. I'd been up to London every now and then, but I wasn't used to big cities, and I suddenly found myself thrown into this.

My friend in the Bronx didn't really know anybody any more. She'd been away at college, so for the first few days it was just very ordinary, looking at museums and things. Then after I'd been there for a week, her brother took us along to a party he'd been invited to. That party changed everything. It was held in a penthouse in Manhattan to launch a pop group and it was absolutely amazing. They had a woman there whom I'd heard about from art college. She was playing a harp and you cut off her clothes as she played, so she ended up playing the harp in the nude. This was the time of happenings and all that kind of thing. I thought I'd really arrived. I met some designers at this party and within three days I had moved out of the Bronx and was living in the Village.

The Village was a really exciting place to be then. There was a feeling of freedom, which was something that I had never quite experienced before. It was totally different. I was experimenting with all sorts of things, including drugs. I took Acid for the first time. Oh, it was so totally different for me. At college it had been much more a drinking than a drug scene. There were drugs around, but I don't think they were around very much. It was only in my last year, in about 1968, or 1969, that younger students started to bring the whole drug thing in – and then they weren't very good drugs either.

I'd only tried them on one occasion. I remember meeting this one particular friend, a boy, who I think influenced me more than anybody else at that time. He was a really good friend and he said, 'Look, you really ought to try drugs,' so I did. But they didn't do anything for me. I wasn't a smoker and I didn't know how to inhale. It was only hash and it affected me very little. Only when I went to the States did the whole drug thing hit me. It was so much bigger over there. I went for three months. I went out looking like this nice, rather conventional, well-brought-up girl and I came back looking, I suppose, a bit of a hippy.

In America, once I'd moved away from the Bronx and got used to things there, I began to meet so many interesting people. I would just walk around and talk to people that I met. There's this thing about communication in the States. It happens more than it does here, and at the time I was so open. I just loved new impressions. New impressions were so important to me. I would allow myself to walk into situations that now I would be absolutely horror-struck by. I was really so naïve. I could have got myself into serious trouble, but I was very trusting and that trust carried me through into fantastic places. You know, I would go out with a group of people and we would just wander around and talk to people and have experiences.

We weren't 'high' all the time, but it carried us through. It sort of sustained us. It opened you up to so many things. I met this Swedish flute player, who was almost like a twin soul, and I moved into the flat where he lived. There was a communication between us that I hadn't experienced before. We were just so close together in terms of our minds. I often think that there are certain people that you meet and you really get a connection with them that you can't describe, and it happened to me with that particular person. It was so totally different from anything I'd known. All this was really starting to change me. I wrote lots of righteous letters to my parents telling them how much I had woken up, though of course I didn't say how I had reached this state.

I went travelling. I went travelling over to the west coast and back on a Greyhound bus ticket. I'd get on a bus and I wouldn't even know where I was going. I would just go in a certain direction. When I got out I would have arrived in a town that I had never even thought of going to. Sometimes I would ask people, 'Where's the place to go,' and they might say, 'The place you *don't* go is such-and-such an area.' Then I'd know that there was *the* place to go. It wasn't necessarily that safe, but it was most probably exciting.

I wouldn't do anything like that now, but then I never thought about the danger. I once arrived in a town, somewhere I think in North Carolina, and somehow I found myself in an all-black community. I stayed there for two or three days. I was the only white person and somebody gave me a hotel room. Somebody actually paid for the hotel room, and if a man pays for a hotel room it is usually because he wants something. But this man – I think he owned a hairdressing salon – just bought me a hotel room! I think I went past his place and he must have said, 'Hello,' and I said, 'Hello,' and we got talking. As I said before, people are so much more open in the States – or I think they were at that particular time – and anyway, I would simply do things like that then. So I ended up in a hotel room free and was taken along to clubs, black clubs. There I was, sort of being part of this, yet also very much aware that I was really outside it all at the same time, just 'recording' it. I was just taking it in, simply collecting new experiences.

This was the time of the Civil Rights Movement in America, but I can't really remember much about that. What I do remember, though, about being in this place in North Carolina is that I understood a lot more about what it was like to be black. I hadn't come into contact with very many black people before, and I wasn't really very aware of the extent of racial prejudice. I think all I'd heard was one anti-Semitic remark at the time of Suez, when I must have been very young, but otherwise I wasn't aware of anything else.

In fact, apart from having been bound up with what was going on in Israel, I was really very naïve then about most social and political issues. I think I'd first realised at art college that I wasn't really a very political person, in contrast to those who were. The Student Union activists seemed more involved in politics than they were in creating their work. I think one of them did actually go off and become a union official in a large factory. Seeing people like this who were so committed, just made me realise what a wishy-washy person I was politically.

We had one demonstration at art college, but I can't even remember what we were demonstrating about, and

I'm not sure I really knew even then! I think it was in sympathy with the student occupation of the art college at Hornsey. There was some connection between Hornsey and Cardiff at the time. I also remember the Paris student riots of 1968 happening, and I couldn't understand why some of the other students were so worked up about it all. Then there was Vietnam. I was in London on the day of that very big demonstration in Grosvenor Square. I'd come down on a college trip that, looking back, had probably been organised so that people who did want to take part could be there. But I didn't go anywhere near the Square. Before the actual demonstration there was a march, which I think started in Trafalgar Square. Anyway, I know there was some kind of enormous parade before they ended up in Grosvenor Square, and standing there just watching bits of it made me realise that I wasn't really that committed to any one cause.

Actually, it was only when I was in America that I began to feel very strongly about things like Vietnam. I had felt completely divorced from it until I went there and saw how it was affecting people. Before that, I'd always thought that if there was a war and someone was attacking your country, you should stand up and fight. But all the time I was in America, I would hear about the awful things that were going on over in Vietnam, about people being killed, including civilians who weren't directly involved in the conflict. It just seemed so unnecessary. For some reason, the whole peace and anti-war business that was going around at the time hit me in a very emotional way. I began to see how nationalism, this thing about your country being the best and having the right to tell others how to run their affairs, could be so damaging. In America in 1969, the whole nationalistic thing was so apparent with all the flags flying and the rah-rah America bit. It just turned my stomach. I reacted in a way that I never thought I could react. I felt myself to be much more like a citizen of the world for the first time, because I thought to see yourself as a citizen of a particular country could be so destructive.

Talking of peace and love and all that, as part of my trip, I went to California. There I was in California in 1969, with the whole San Francisco and flower power thing going on, and as usual I just met somebody. Again, it was simply one of those things, something that always happened to me in America. I think somebody introduced me to him in San Francisco. We went to Big Sur, which is the area just below San Francisco, between there and LA. It's where the Esalen Institute, the Growth Potential movement place, is. Anyway, it's quite beautiful and had a reputation for being a really special place. He parked the car and we sat looking at it all from the long grass – we just sat there, staring, for about five hours. In fact, if I remember, it was him that introduced me to psilocybin, magic mushrooms. I actually believe now, looking back on it, that he was probably a drug dealer. I know that he had a gun in the car.

All these experiences were so different from the life I had come from in Cardiff, but I wasn't thrown by them at all. They changed me, changed my outlook, but I wasn't frightened or shocked. I was just more open to new things. I really enjoyed America. Most of the time I felt very happy there. I got on with people so easily. They seemed to like me. It was so different to be somewhere and be liked for simply being *me*. If you've always lived in a place where everybody knows you, you don't know how much of getting on with people is just familiarity. But when you go to a totally new place for the first time and have to make friends and people seem to like you straight away, then it's very reassuring. Wherever I went in the States, whether it was for a day or for two days or whatever, people would be asking me if I wanted to stay. They were sure they could find me a job working as an art instructress in some place. In each case, it was quite tempting, but I just don't think I was ready to make such an enormous change.

When I first came back, I went home for a bit. But I had already decided, even at art college, that I couldn't stay in Cardiff. My whole outlook had changed so much. I no longer shared my parents' values, though at the same time I didn't want them to change. I could see that there was no point in them changing. I knew I had to move away and I was quite lucky. My parents had a friend who had a flat in London. He was a businessman who worked in Cardiff. He only used his London flat at weekends and he said that I could live there, so I did.

There I was in London at the end of the sixties, with a whole flat – most of the time, all to myself. It was extraordinary! The only restriction was that I couldn't bring people back as much as I would have liked to. It was just round the corner from this night club, where there was music going on every night – and good people playing, too. I got to know the people who ran it, which meant I could go in free. I would arrive about half-past ten at night, and just stay for hours. It was great, really great.

Everybody else in my year had done a very safe thing. They had done a teaching course after their degree, but I wouldn't do it. I mean, I couldn't do it. I knew I couldn't do it. I wanted to show my work and I was naïve enough to think that could happen – and, in a strange way, all my dreams came true. I actually was lucky enough to show my work, and to go on television talking about it, and to have magazine articles written about me. I never would have believed that that was possible, but it was.

That was a very strange time, the end of the sixties and beginning of the seventies. Somehow, if you had enough belief in yourself, it felt as though you could do anything. It's so much more difficult now, more tangled up with money, just having enough to survive. I never thought about how I would make a living then. I think that was partly coming from a background where there was always enough money around to be comfortable, and I just never thought about it not being like that. But there wasn't this stress then on careers and a regular job. I never thought about it, and basically I didn't have to.

Eventually I got a job in an art gallery, where I hardly made anything, but then I didn't need to make very much. I had my flat which was rent-free and the man who owned it brought home lots of food at the weekend, so I'd live on that for the rest of the week. I was much skinnier than I am now – seven and a half stone – and I didn't eat very much. I'd make a bit of extra money by selling sandwiches in the club I mentioned. Really, I lived on practically nothing, and I survived.

The gallery I worked in was in Lisle Street. It belonged to the AIA, the Artists' Institute Association, a movement that started in the middle of the 1930s to fight fascism. Angela Flowers had her gallery above it at the time. The AIA and Angela's were absolute one-offs. There was nothing else like that around there, only Chinese restaurants and prostitutes. In fact, people used to come into the gallery because they were waiting for a prostitute. If somebody was already up there with her, they'd come into the AIA and look at the paintings to pass the time.

The job came my way because someone who knew and liked my work and who was on the board of the AIA got me an exhibition at their gallery. I then continued to work there. I just did everything because I fell into it, not because I planned to do anything. I came down to London simply because I wanted to get out of Cardiff, and the flat was there and that was it. I knew I wanted to show my work, but I never thought about how I would get started. Somewhere along the way it just happened.

In Cardiff, a lot of the art college crowd used to go to the city's one and only jazz club, so there was a whole group of people around the art and music scene who all knew one another. I'd really lost touch with most of them, but somehow certain links remained. When I first came up to London, a jazz musician who I first met in Cardiff looked after me and took me to Ronnie Scott's almost every night. That's how I got to know a lot of people. I never thought of myself as having 'arrived', as having got into some really trendy, arty scene, though I suppose it was a bit like that. It was like a strange dream, being part of it all, having this exhibition, working at the gallery and mixing with all these creative people. There were always artists and such traipsing through the gallery to visit Angela. You had to go through the AIA gallery to get to her gallery. One day this woman came to see her, walked through the AIA gallery, saw my exhibition, and liked it. She was organising an exhibition at the ICA at the time and asked me if I would like to take part in it.

The exhibition at the ICA was something called *Ten Sitting Rooms*. Ten artists had been invited to present their interpretation of a sitting-room. This was 1971 and the ICA was going through a really low period. They wanted to have a showpiece that would attract a lot of publicity, and this was it. For several of us, it was our first major exhibition. Patrick Hughes did something, and one of the then unknowns was the guy who organises the Alternative Miss World thing – Andrew Logan. He had the next room to me and had little tea parties there in the afternoons. I remember hearing him on the radio years later, and he'd obviously made it. He'd just had one of his Miss World things, and here I was sitting at home with a baby and I thought 'Oh God!' Ten years earlier we'd been sort of part of the same creative world. Now our lives were so different.

The end of the sixties and early seventies was a wonderful period for me. It almost felt as if there was a wave of freedom sweeping through certain parts of the world at that time. It was like a minor Renaissance. There was just so much energy around. There was this great sense of possibility. I tend to wonder if one loses that and gets more set as one gets older, or whether that energy just isn't around now. If it is, it is all so tied up with making money. There isn't the same freedom. It's very sad. Though I do sometimes think it would have been better if we'd been a little bit more aware of some things. When I left art college, I felt that somehow the people who had put us through this whole education didn't complete it. We could have had more at the end, more education on how we could have used our talents to earn our living, other than just teaching. For example, I could have developed something from my environments that I could have actually sold. I could have made cushions or furnishings perhaps, things that were a sort of carry on from that. But we were never taught about business know-how. It just didn't seem to be important then.

But I still say that it's a shame that the energy and feeling that you could do anything you wanted to do in the late sixties doesn't seem to be present now. I'm definitely glad I was the age I was then, though I'm sure everybody says that. Most people wouldn't change the years in which they were young and everything was developing. Maybe there are exceptions. I mean, look at the people that the sixties didn't touch because their upbringing was so straight that they couldn't allow themselves to be touched. I can see that it had to happen later on. I have one particular friend, who is only eighteen months older than I am, and yet she stuck so much to the lines that she was supposed to that only when she reached 40 did she really rebel. She gave up her marriage and started to do some of the things that I basically did in my late teens or early twenties.

There was a mass of people who were brought up in the same way as I was, went to the same school as I did, but who weren't affected at all by the changes of the sixties. That sense of freedom just didn't touch them, and that was the vast majority of people I knew. I don't know about London, but I know that in Cardiff it affected the tiniest, tiniest minority of people – people at the art college and a few people around the university. I know so few people who went through that particular thing, that change that came with the sixties that gave a totally different way of looking at things – basically, a freaky way of looking at things. I came out of 1969 into 1970 feeling as though I had entered a different world. I was very much more aware of things on different levels. It was moving away from being aware of just oneself to being aware of the world, and things beyond the world as well.

For me, going to the States was the biggest push into that new sense of consciousness and awareness that was starting to happen in the late sixties. The whole drug culture that was opening up there made me realise that there were possibilities of reaching out into other dimensions that I had not thought existed before. Some people took things like Acid and just saw pretty colours and that was fine, but for me it was more than that. I went through cosmic experiences that completely changed me. Later, back in London, I remember one particular Acid trip. I was with a friend, who recognised that there was something in me that I had not yet reached and she was pushing me towards it. Anyway, we took far more Acid than we probably should, and it felt like I was dying and being reborn. I saw things that I could never ever express. Even now I can't get to that level of what it was I saw, but it definitely changed my whole idea about spirits and souls and all of those things, and eventually led to me becoming interested in mysticism and spirituality.

All this wasn't just about getting heavily into drugs for their own sake. I knew people who were like that, but I never thought of buying or possessing drugs myself. They were just generally around at parties and things. Smoking dope was part of being sociable. It was just part of the culture that I was in. For many of us, drugs were a way of looking for something, a different way of seeing and thinking. I don't think we really knew exactly what, but I know a lot of friends who experienced something very special in the sixties and even into the seventies, when the whole spiritual movement was growing out of what had happened in the sixties. The thing about the sixties was that it was an expansion, an expansion of our viewpoint.

I think the sixties delivered an enormous amount, and in some ways we've just messed bits of it up. We were terribly naïve. It's very odd now when you think about some of the ideas that came through then, and how they have just been shoved under the carpet. There have been all these programmes about how people thought in the sixties, how they thought the world was going to change and how they thought it was going to be so totally different, but instead what's happened is that many people have gradually become more and more like their parents, in terms of carrying on with 'straight' jobs and retaining very similar values.

I know we can't go back to exactly the way it was then. We've all got responsibilities now – houses, families, and all that sort of thing. And I wouldn't want to lose any of that. I wouldn't want to be as I was, but there must be a way of retaining what we have now and still giving our minds the space to expand. The lives of so many people I know have now fallen into a cosy, closed-in pattern. Though there is one big difference about it all that always strikes me, and that is that most of the women I know are now working. Even the Jewish princess, who wasn't ever supposed to work after she got married, has got herself a job – out of boredom, not because she needs the money.

I wasn't really aware of the Women's Movement in the sixties. I don't think it really took off until the seventies, with Germaine Greer and all that stuff. The seeds of it must have been around at the end of the sixties, but it didn't really touch me. Then it was independence generally that interested me. I thought of rebellion against my parents' ideas for independence as a whole, but not because I was a woman. I think if I had been more aware of Women's Lib, I probably would have had much more of a weapon with which to fight some of the really chauvinistic people at the art college. The atmosphere there was incredibly chauvinistic and I knew then something was wrong, something was really wrong, but I didn't know how to deal with it. I couldn't express what I felt very well and I didn't feel I had anything behind me giving me the power to be able to say to some of these men, 'What the hell do you think you are doing?' I think if more women had been more aware, if the whole women's thing had been more generally talked about then, I would have felt able to say something. Looking back now, I feel very angry at some of the things we had to put up with.

ALEX

I was born in 1951, so I can remember being a teenager in the sixties. In 1963 I was 12 and I seem to remember I'd just about started going to parties. I was definitely very much into that kind of thing – really attracted to it. There would be a party every Saturday night and on the odd Friday night as well, and boys featured in all that to some extent. I'd go to parties and have a little snog in a corner. That's basically what one did at parties – and dance around a bit. But I didn't actually have boyfriends as such at that age.

My parents were rather strict. They had an incredibly traditional attitude towards bringing us up. They were much stricter than the parents of most of my friends. I'd have to be in by 10.30 p.m., whereas other girls I knew could get back at midnight, and there were various places that I wasn't allowed to go. They wouldn't let me go to this place called The Barge in Kingston, which I was extremely keen to go to. This was where Terry, the one who sang the motor-bike song, used to perform as well as various other similar people. But anyway, I was forbidden to go, so I never went there. All my friends did and that really irritated me. I think my parents had heard that drug-taking happened there and they were sort of being protective. In fact I wasn't interested in drugs at this stage, but I certainly wanted to know the kind of people who went to The Barge and I felt extremely left out at not knowing them.

I couldn't wait to get out and rebel, but at 13 I went away to boarding school. My father was travelling a lot at the time and it was nice for my mother to be able to go with him rather than staying behind to look after my brother and me. I think it was a question of either staying with our grandparents while they were away or going to boarding school and as I'd been down for this place since I was a child, I went.

I quite enjoyed the first term. I made friends quite easily. It was quite nice to have friends around all the time. We had midnight feasts – oh yes, they really did happen – and raided the kitchen at night. But obviously there were no boys and no parties or anything else like that. When I came home for Christmas after the first term, I can remember feeling a bit left out. I felt terribly cut off from most of my old friends who all seemed to have been having a great time while I was away. I was invited out to parties and all the rest of it, but various people would be there who I didn't know and I no longer felt one of the group at all.

By the end of my first year, I was pretty convinced, although I had a lot of fun in some ways, that I wanted to go back to day school. I really did feel I was missing out on more amusing things. But it was agreed that I shouldn't move until I had taken my O-levels, which seemed fair enough, though my main memory of the next couple of years at boarding school was of desperately wanting to get out of the place.

It was a completely rarified atmosphere, which doesn't make you particularly aware of what's going on around you in the wider world. It could have been at any time. It wasn't like being in the sixties or not being in the sixties. It was just boarding school – an almost totally female society. We hardly saw any boys or men. There were two male teachers and they were ghastly! None of us liked them. They were old, smelly and unattractive, so none of us were eating our hearts for them.

The school uniform was an absolute nightmare. There was the basic uniform that you wore during school hours and after that you wore what was called 'mufti', meaning your own clothes, but they had to be plain and neat. You certainly couldn't wear jeans or trousers of any description. Then there was Sunday uniform and there was a winter games uniform and a summer games uniform etc., etc. Some concessions were made to fashion, but very, very few. I remember being quite aware of fashion, no doubt about that, but there wasn't a lot one could do with a school uniform. There was no question of wearing any kind of mini-skirt. Two inches above your knees was about the limit. We weren't really allowed to wear make-up either, but we did sometimes dabble with the odd bit of mascara.

I was never particularly involved with my school work. It was just something I had to do, so I got on with it. I never found it particularly difficult. I had a lot of friends and was much more interested in having fun, which at a boarding school usually involved breaking some rule or other. I think the most daring thing we did was to meet boys from the local grammar at the bottom of the school field. That's the kind of thing I was really interested in. In fact, work took second place to everything else. But as far as I'm concerned life really started when I left boarding school at 15. Everything really started happening then. That must have been 1966.

I went back to the school I'd been at before, which was near where we lived in Putney, so I was quite close to the centre of London. It was very easy to get in and out and I'd regularly go to the King's Road and back of a Saturday. It was straight through on the train from Putney. There were wonderful clothes shops there then. It was one of the best places to buy clothes and there were all these trendy people around. I really liked it. I also went to Carnaby Street a few times, but it hasn't made so much of an impression on me, apart from, of course, the name. I don't remember spending much time there.

By this time I was doing A-levels, but I don't remember spending a lot of time working for them. Of course, I did do some work, but I'd chosen to do pure and applied maths and physics, which aren't exactly heavy memorising subjects. You've either got a knack for them or you haven't. I always did well in exams, although I did sometimes get anxious about them. I can remember taking one set of exams and thinking I'd done so badly that I burst into tears afterwards. Then it turned out I'd done really well. But generally school work was never a problem. The real focus of my life was getting out and being part of whatever was going on at the time on the social scene. I was much more interested in that. Work had to be done and at times I'd even get quite into it and start enjoying it, but it was never at the centre of things for me.

I could go out on schoolday nights as well as at weekends, but I certainly wasn't allowed out every night. I'd got to know quite a few local boys, usually through my brother, and I often went out with one of them. Some of them had motor-bikes. We might go to the cinema and on Saturdays there would always be a party somewhere. Kingston was quite a small centre in those days. Of course, these were never all-night parties. I had to get back home before my 'curfew' hour and my parents would always insist on meeting any boy I went out with. There was never any chance of sneaking out and staying out until three in the morning. The only time I did stay out longer than my curfew – I think I had probably graduated to midnight on a Saturday night by then – I walked in at about ten past twelve and my parents had already informed the police!

The highlight of the week from when I was about 16 to 17 was going to this place called The Toby Jug in Surbiton. It was a pub and there were all these fantastic people who played there – John Mayall, Captain Beefheart, Chicken Shack, Fleetwood Mac. They were all regulars then, before some of them got really big. A few friends and I went there every Wednesday without fail and met loads of these semi-freako types. Most of them had left school and were already working, so generally they were a bit older then us. They were what I thought of then as super groovy people, usually with long hair and really trendy clothes. They were definitely the sort of people that interested me, much more than studious, short-haired, pimply youths. I thought it was all super glamorous and we usually had a fantastic evening. There'd always be plenty of people you could talk to and I made lots of friends there.

I think a lot of the people at The Toby Jug were smoking dope, though I didn't get into dope or drugs of any kind until I was 18 and had left school. That was when I had a flat of my own for a while just before going to university. Of course, the opportunity had been there before but I just hadn't taken it. There must have been drugs at some of the concerts I used to go off to around London in my last year at school. A lot of these concerts were at the Roundhouse. There was often stuff going on all night there then, which I wouldn't have been allowed to go to, but you could get drugs there at any time. It's funny, but I wasn't at all tempted at that point. I can remember this guy telling me, some time around then, that I'd be having sex and taking drugs and all the rest of it pretty soon and I can remember saying 'Oh no, I'll never do that kind of thing.' Obviously, I didn't intend to get into all that. I just fell into bad ways later on!

I never seemed to have any money. I always spent it all as soon as I got it, mainly on going out and on records and clothes. I can certainly remember buying some of the The Beatles' records. I think they once played locally at Wimbledon Palais, but that was probably when my parents would have considered me too young to go to a Beatles' concert. I was much more of a fan of The Rolling Stones, right from the early days, though I still thought The Beatles were fantastic as well. I went through phases of fancying all of them except for Ringo – Paul was my first favourite, then George and then John, and John then remained the favourite. Oh and I can remember, before I went to boarding school in fact, when I must have been just 12 or 13, there were these Beatles cards that came in some kind of sweets, bubblegum I think. Anyway I hated the bubblegum but I'd buy the wretched stuff to get all these cards, which we swopped at school in order to get a complete set.

My parents had given me a clothes allowance since I was 13 and I seemed to spend most of this on picking up lots of very small pieces of material. Remnants would be enough for making up mini-skirts. I used to make most of my skirts myself then and the great thing about them being really really short was that you didn't have to pay much for the material. You could make a skirt for just a few shillings, so I managed to have quite a lot of skirts, all very, very short indeed. Of course, at boarding school, as I've said, we had to wear uniform, but outside and later on I always wore extremely short skirts. I can remember one holiday I was going on, when I was 15 or 16 I think, and my parents wouldn't let me go in what they called this 'terribly short skirt'. They were really furious about it. Some of my skirts were, because they were hipsters in those days, only 8 or 10 inches long. I can remember measuring them.

I don't remember ever feeling cold in mini-skirts, so I must have worn tights with them in winter – in summer I wouldn't have worn anything on my legs. I think I can remember sheer tights being available from about 1967 or 1968. Maybe they were around earlier. I'm not exactly sure. When I was about 12 or 13, I'd sometimes worn stockings, but suspenders would have looked horrendous with a really short skirt. I can also remember those things that held themselves up. They had stretchy tops and you couldn't be too fat to wear them which, fortunately, I wasn't. I may have worn those for a while, but I'm certain tights were around by the time I was 15 or 16.

Anyway, fashion and records must have been the main things I spent my money on and, of course, a bit of make-up. What else would a girl spend her money on, I would like to know? Yes, I was very keen on make-up, not so much on my face but certainly the heavy black liner around my eyes. Once, when my mother had been out shopping, I went to meet her at the station and she came out, took one look at me and said, 'For heavens sake, you look like a tart!'

Some of my money while I was still at school came from Saturday and holiday jobs. My parents were actually quite generous, but one or two of my friends were getting Saturday jobs, so I thought I'd do it too. I worked about three Saturdays in Woolworth's, then gave that up as really dire. I got a fantastic job at a zoo, over one summer when I must have been about 16. There was a complete kid's section there with a lot of boys running things like the helter-skelters and the trains. These boys were great fun. They must have been about 16 or 17 or perhaps even older and they were nearly all clad in leather and rode motor-bikes. I suppose you would have called them rockers, as in mods and rockers.

These boys were so amusing. Though once, disastrously, they invited me to a party. I took a friend of mine and a couple of them turned up on their motor-bikes to pick us up. Anyway, it turned out that we were the only girls there and they took us into a bedroom of this large empty house – somebody's parents had probably gone away – and we sat on the bed. Then about half a dozen or more of these boys just got on top of us. They were only young kids really but it was still quite frightening. They didn't pull our knickers off or anything like that, but we really freaked out, so the guys who'd brought us along just stopped it all and took us off at that point. Further social- ising was not had with that lot!

But basically the zoo job was great. I was mainly selling ice creams. I ate a hell of a lot of ice cream that summer, I can tell you. However, I didn't eat much else and if I'd really eaten a lot one day, I'd starve the next. I had this thing about being really slim. I must have been pretty near anorexic. I liked to eat about two pieces of fruit for break- fast, two for lunch and then perhaps a bit of meat and veg excluding potatoes in the evening. And I'd measure the number of cups of tea and coffee I could have, which was five, spaced throughout the day. That was my normal diet. Of course, I would break this now and again but it managed to keep me jolly skinny, the way I liked to be. I even went through a period of sort of binging, but not really the serious binging that you read about, and I stopped having regular periods.

All this business with food went back to when I was at boarding school. I'd put on quite a bit of weight when I was first there. One of the main excitements of life at boarding school was eating and I was introduced to these extra- ordinary habits. People there could be quite nutty about food. I can remember we'd sit at the table in the evening and there would be various different spreads, one of which was this chocolate spread, which these girls would mash up with butter and sugar and then put onto their bread. I was fascinated by this at first. So many girls got into these gross eating habits and I soon learnt too, with the result that I put on weight.

I didn't suddenly become hugely fat, but I was fatter than I'd ever been before. I'd always been reasonably skinny before that and it quickly dawned on me that I didn't like being podgy, so I went on a diet. I did it with a friend. We both went on a diet and virtually starved. I really found it quite easy to do. In fact, I think I enjoyed it. I really enjoyed getting thinner and thinner, and I didn't feel hungry. I lost 10 pounds probably in two or three weeks. I can remember my parents being worried when they came to visit me on a school outing, because there had definitely been a bit of puppy fat on me one minute and then suddenly there I was, almost a stone lighter. I probably went up to nine or perhaps nine and a half stone, which was fat for me, and then very quickly I got quite slim. Anyway I was delighted and that must have established my want-to-be-thin obsession, which continued for a long time afterwards.

I went on another massive diet when I first got back to day school, but I wasn't yet anorexic by that stage. I was just keen on being slim and I kept going on these diets and somehow managed to get slimming pills from the doctor. They worked like a dream and I got slightly hooked on them. I must have been 16 then and there was a slimming pill scenario on and off with me for a hell of a long time after that. I loved taking them. They gave me such a buzz and I never felt hungry. I got used to not eating. I was quite obsessed with it all. I can remember losing fantastic amounts of weight. I was so skinny, but it was the Twiggy era and I thought that was great.

My parents got pretty concerned about all this. My mother couldn't stand the doctor down the road, because he gave me these slimming pills. She was absolutely furious. It drove her bananas and because my periods were all messed up, they were worried about my ovaries.

I'd never really had regular periods, even before all this, but I was sent for tests and eventually they diagnosed anorexia nervosa. I wasn't a serious case and I certainly didn't have bulimia and all that make-yourself-sick kind of business, so I wasn't sent for any special treatment. But it was an issue for a hell of a long time after that. My parents really watched me, but I don't think I was particularly concerned. At that point I think that at least half of my female friends had what I would call anorexia to some degree.

I don't think all this obsession with being thin was just fashion – Twiggy and so on. I think it was largely to do with feeling attractive and I definitely did feel more attractive when I was really skinny. The world and all the boys at the party would be mine, I felt, when I was thin. And so they were. They hadn't shown nearly so much interest when I was a bit chubby, I can assure you. I had lots of boyfriends around that time, though none of them were what you'd call serious. Sometimes I'd go out with several at the same time and none ever lasted all that long. They were just friends really. I was never madly in love or anything like that. I just liked them. I had fun with them and I liked having lots of them around, paying me plenty of attention. There was one, though, who I got rather keen on and I went out with him for maybe two or three months. I can't remember how it all ended. I think that he started doing his A-levels and working more and more and more and I wasn't exactly the sort to sit at home and hold his hand while he studied hard. I was off finding more amusing pastures.

I was never the romantic type. I had passions for people but they were quickly spent. Perhaps I'd have a passion for someone for a week or two, then I'd be in love with the next one. I'd get bored terribly quickly. I certainly wasn't looking for a 'Mr Right' at that stage. I don't think many teenagers ever are, though there were various friends of mine who went out with the same bloke for three months, six months or even a year. I thought they must be out of their minds, quite honestly. I definitely wasn't looking for deep relationships. I was in there to have fun.

Generally the boys I went out with would be a couple of years older than me and my parents were absolutely fine about it all. They were quite happy for these boys to be about the house, wandering in and out. I don't think it bothered them in the slightest. In fact, they probably thought it was quite healthy that there were all these chaps around. But they certainly liked to know who they were. Some were friends of my brother. Generally it was all right if it was a respectable lad, say from the local school, who they had shaken hands with. The only one I can remember them really taking exception to, probably because he was so much older, was the one I was most proud to have in the house. He was one of the pop singers I had met at The Toby Jug. It turned out that this bloke was married and, although I didn't actually have an affair with him or anything like that, I later met two or three girls who did. He was obviously having a whale of a time. But anyway my father threw him out of the house or rather he told him it was time to go and started as though he was going to take no nonsense.

There was no real sex in these relationships, just a lot of heavy petting. Usually there would be a bit of kissing and tongue in the mouth stuff and then they might try and rip off your bra. I wouldn't have any of that though, because I was very embarrassed at having such minute tits. It wasn't prudishness, I just didn't want them to feel and realise how little there was there. I've always on and off had a complex about having small breasts. Even when small breasts were fashionable in the late sixties, I still had a bit of a complex. I sometimes used to feel that I couldn't ever be really sexy with small breasts. I even used to think about getting enough money to have plastic surgery.

I didn't really get into sex until I was about 18 or 19, when I'd finally left home, which was more like in the early seventies. The first time was with a bloke I was going out with. It wasn't planned and we hadn't intended it to happen. It just did. For a while I just couldn't imagine having sex with anybody else, but that didn't last.

However, while I was still at school, there was never any question in my mind – I certainly didn't want to go around having sex with blokes. I think till you've actually had sex in the first place, you don't really know what you're missing anyway. There were various people in my form at school who used 'to go the whole way' or whatever we called it at the time and I used to think they were definitely rather tarty.

Several of the girls I knew were on the Pill and my aunt, who was a family planning doctor, saw some of them in her clinic. I think she used to give the Pill to girls who were just going to do it anyway and would otherwise get pregnant. Her preferred solution was definitely that they didn't do it in the first place. She would certainly have been horrified if her own daughter or niece had turned up at the clinic, though I did go on the Pill at one point for a completely different reason – to regulate my periods. That was when I was 15 or 16 and I didn't feel at all well on it, so I stopped. I didn't try it again until I was at university. I'd go on it on and off, but really I hated it. I absolutely hated it. It made me feel awful. I'd be on it for a few months at a time, but I was never somebody who'd be on it year in, year out.

Sex was never something that was particularly discussed openly in our house. My mother told me the facts of life in a clinical kind of way when I was about 12, but that was about it. My father never mentioned the subject. I've no idea what my brother got up to, if anything. He was pretty shy really, although he would occasionally tell me the odd smutty joke. In fact relationships in our family were rather polite generally, sometimes even a little formal. There was never a lot of discussion about anything. They didn't even discuss our future much. It was just assumed that we would go to university and get a good education and probably have some sort of career, but there was never any great pressure to achieve. They did try, however, to make me think about what I wanted to do. I can remember computers being talked about and someone saying that you could make lots of money like that, but I didn't understand about money at all then. I went through the sixties and most of the seventies thinking 'money stinks', meanwhile taking lots of it from my parents! I think it was always clear that much as I put my parents down for being materialistic and so on, I was in fact the most materialistic person in our family. But I didn't realise that then.

I wasn't particularly conscious of the way things were changing for women in terms of jobs and expectations in the sixties, either. The Women's Movement and politics generally meant very little to me. At that stage it never occurred to me that I might have any problems because I was a woman. I'd been to an all-girls school, my mother and several of my aunts were professionals and there appeared to be complete equality as human beings between my mother and my father. Women in my family, especially on my father's side had been doing things outside the home for generations. Even my grandmother had been to university. I don't think it would have occurred to me to think that women were anything less than equal.

Anyway, I finished my A-levels, got a place at university and then decided to take a year off. It was a wonderful year. Towards the end of it I got into what I now call my 'sex and drugs and rock 'n' roll' phase, although it wasn't quite as wild as that phrase implies ... and I had the odd job thrown in here and there. Funnily enough my first job was with Richard Branson. My father saw this ad in the paper for selling magazines and it turned out to be Richard Branson and his *Student* magazine, so I went and worked there. I must have been the only virgin around, literally. I fell terribly in love with ... well not terribly in love, but I had a brief, little sort of passion for this guy there and I remember him saying to me, when we met again years later, how bored he got with this incessant snogging we had to do because I wouldn't have sex. I think everybody else there was having a hell of a lot of it.

I was only there, in fact, for a couple of months. Branson was a real live wire, always doing this, that and the other. Looking back, I can see why he has done so well. He was really dynamic, zapping around doing his thing. And all the people I met there, they all seemed so super cool as if they'd got it all worked out. I felt I was the only one who hadn't. I felt terribly uncool. But I had a great time. It was fun. I got taken to some really super trendy parties, where there must have been a lot of dope around, but at this stage I still wasn't into it. In fact, somehow I remained pretty innocent and naive during the whole time I was working for Branson. Initially, I was still living at home, but then I briefly moved into this large house with several other girls. However, I didn't end up staying there very long, because I had to share a room with this girl who would sometimes bring her boyfriend back and have sex in the bed next to mine. Well, there was me, a little virgin, and I just didn't want to know. I found it absolutely revolting. I was never that liberated!

Moving away from home meant I now needed a bit more money, so I got another job, in the Chelsea Drug Store on the King's Road. The Chelsea Drug Store was a bit like a covered market, a sort of complex of various different boutiques and shops and there was a bar and a café and that kind of thing. It was a very trendy little spot. I sold ice cream and fizzy drinks. I had my own little kiosk looking out onto the street, so I saw the world go by and got to know lots of people there. Sometimes we used to go to this really trendy pub at lunchtime, where there would be all these super-cool drug dealers. As I've said, I wasn't yet into any of that, but if any of these dealers thought the police were onto them, they would come and dump their weights of dope on innocent me in my ice cream kiosk and I was so naïve I'd just take them. It never even occurred to me that I could get caught with the stuff!

There were concerts in Hyde Park that summer. I must have gone to several, but I can't really remember if that was all over one summer or whether there were some the following year as well. Anyway, The Stones were there in 1969. I can definitely remember going to that one and thinking it was great. There were all these wonderful people to look at, exotic creatures, scantily clad hippy types and it was summer and warm and all this fantastic music was beating out. Some people were snogging and cuddling, but I wasn't aware of people actually having sex in the middle of the park! If they were, I didn't see it. It was mainly sitting around. It was just an amazing scene.

I suppose I was sort of a hippy then. What I mean was I was wearing hippyish clothes, but I wasn't into the more extreme stuff, like painting flowers and things all over my body. A lot of people, to some extent, looked a bit hippyish then. I'd wear these long crushed velvet skirts and jackets and jumble sale-type stuff with loads and loads of beads of every description. I had stacks of beads. I'd probably wear a hat, a floppy hat, as well, but I never really went in for bare feet because it was too uncomfortable. I usually wore sandals instead.

By the time summer was over, I'd finished with both the Richard Branson set-up and the café. Then my A-level results came out and I'd got As in all my subjects, so everyone kept saying that I should try for Oxford and Cambridge which didn't seem like a bad idea at the time. I suppose there was a bit of parental pressure and I just sort of went along the line of least resistance. I went back to live at home, but I did the work for the Oxbridge exams at this crammer near Marble Arch, so I was still coming into London every day and there were some really quite amusing people there. I did the exams and got interviews. I was supposed to be going up to read PPE at Oxford and I hadn't got a clue about anything to do with politics, philosophy or economics, so needless to say, I didn't go down too well. But if Oxford didn't want to know about me, Cambridge did. However, I'd somehow gone off the whole Oxbridge idea by now. I decided that I wanted to go somewhere a bit more modern and, as I already knew quite a few people at Sussex, I applied and got in there.

Meanwhile, in the summer before I went to university I moved into this flat near World's End. This was the summer of 1970 and I was there for about three or four months. I shared it with a girlfriend, who I'd been with at the crammer. It was just a one-bedroom flat, but it could be two bedrooms because there was a large hall which we put a mattress down in. Sometimes I slept in the hall while my friend had the bedroom and then we'd change around every now and again. It cost something like £8 a week for the whole flat. I got the money by doing the odd job here and there and my father also paid me a small allowance, something like £15 a month, because in theory I was supposed to be spending that summer preparing myself to go to university – reading and that kind of thing.

That flat was where I really got into dope and other drugs for the first time. Though I think I'd smoked my first joint just before that. I can't remember exactly when that was, but it must certainly have been after I'd done the Oxbridge exams. I bumped into this bloke I knew. He was living with his brother and I went to their 'den', where they actually taught me how to inhale. I smoked this joint and for the first time got smashed. I must say it was hilarious fun. From then on I started smoking properly, inhaling and getting stoned. I obviously got addicted to tobacco from inhaling these joints, because I think I started smoking cigarettes as well at about the same time.

There was quite a scene centred around our flat. People would just turn up at any time. There would often be eight or ten people around there and we'd stay up all night, all tripping out and smoking dope. I can remember my first trip. It was late at night, and I was probably already stoned. I was a bit nervous about doing it, but some bloke had just flown in from America and he'd got some mescaline, which everybody said was the purest stuff they'd ever had and that it was just wonderful. So I thought that if it was the most pure and wonderful stuff, I'd do some too. Everybody there was doing it, so I took some and sure enough it was brilliant. It was absolutely brilliant. It was just *mind-blowingly, blissfully wonderful.* That set me off. A lot of people I knew used to have bad trips, but I never did. I thought it was the most wonderful ecstatic thing. It would be different at different times. I'd have these almost spiritual trips sometimes when I was on my own. Then, there'd be other trips which would be purely sensual, but I thought they were all fantastic.

I don't ever remember any legal or money hassles with getting hold of dope and stuff. A hell of a lot of the people I knew around me were wheeling and dealing in a small way and sometimes I would get dope from them for other people. But I was never into any real dealing myself. I certainly wasn't interested in making money that way, not with the risks involved. I had that much sense to be paranoid. I probably spent the odd two or three quid on it here and there – there were quid deals in those days – but never the kind of money you'd have to save up for.

One of the big advantages of knowing some of these druggy types was that so many of them seemed to have the kind of contacts for getting hold of tickets for rock concerts. I loved rock music at the time. In fact, I would go as far as saying that I was pretty devoted to it, though I wasn't a fanatical follower of anybody in particular. I just liked lots of different rock types. If somebody good was playing at, say Earl's Court, which was quite local for me, I'd be there. I saw Pink Floyd there and the guy who was always going through lots of different phases, Ziggy Stardust and all that ... David Bowie, though perhaps that was later on.

Going to university at the end of that summer was really more of the same. I already knew various people at Sussex and had been there a few times. One was an old friend whom I'd know since I was a child and he was at the centre of this fantastic dope scene when he was there. He knew all the right people and was definitely a good person to know. I had a great time. I hardly ever went to any lectures and I must have only written about two essays in all.

However, I was only there a year. Towards the end of the summer before what would have been my second year, I became quite ill. My illness was nothing to do with drugs, but I had a lot of time to think and I decided that if I was going to be at university at all, I might as well get a decent degree. By then I had missed the beginning of the new term and as I'd never really got into my course properly – for obvious reasons – I decided it would be better to start again. So I applied for and got a place at London for the following year. Of course, I knew that it would mean starting all over again, doing the complete three years, but that never bothered me. I didn't worry at that stage about getting on with a career. That was the last thing on my mind. It just didn't occur to me to think about such things. A lot of people were like that then. There just seemed to be plenty of jobs and plenty of money around at the end of the sixties and in the early seventies. I never used to think much about the future. I just did my living day by day.

Really I was just very, very easy going. Sometimes I wonder if it would be better now, if I had been a bit more switched on to certain things, like perhaps jobs and money. But then I look at some of the people who did do that kind of thing and they seem sort of 35 going on 55 now. Things were just different for a lot of young people in the sixties. There was a lot more freedom. People were generally into less materialistic things. So at the end of the day, I don't really regret anything I did. I don't think I've ever met anybody who does!

More books from Optima

GROWING UP IN THE FIFTIES by Terry Jordan

Television, teenagers and rock'n'roll
Beatniks, 'Ban the Bomb' and CND
The Coronation and Commonwealth immigration
The New Look ● The Cold War and Suez
Elvis and Buddy Holly ● James Dean

Were the Fifties just nondescript years, a bland transition while the world caught its breath between the excitements of World War II and the Swinging Sixties? *Growing up in the Fifties* proves the Fifties had more to offer than longer skirts and an end to rationing. As the deprivations of the post-war period receded, most people had 'never had it so good' and youth culture was busy inventing itself.

In this collection of seven interviews, girls now grown tell the stories of their childhoods and teen years with perception and humour. Their detailed memories of a daily life, so different from today's, provide a rich background for understanding the events and social attitudes which shaped the decade, the role of women in it, and the individual women they were to become.

ISBN 0 356 15553 6
Price (in UK only) **£5.99**

AGONY COLUMNS by Terry Jordan

Anxious • Lonely • Heartbroken • Confused • Unhappy
Bewildered • Frightened • Naive •

Agony columns provide an outlet for the extremes of human emotion. From the tragic to the trivial, they make public property of private anguish, and in the process, disturb, fascinate and frequently amuse.

Here, Terry Jordan looks back at agony columns over the last 100 years. Her broad selection highlights the conditions, expectations, events and social trends that shaped women's lives. In 1899 a young lady enquires 'what is the fashionable handshake?', while in 1968 a confused mother, who has advised her daughter against sex outside marriage, asks 'am I wrong?'.

The problems remain basically the same, but the advice given reveals the great shifts in social attitudes.

ISBN 0 356 14145 4
Price (in UK only) **£5.95**

WOMEN in WARTIME by Jane Waller and Michael Vaughan-Rees

The unsung heroines of the Second World War were the women who were left behind. Isolated from the action, fearful for the lives of their menfolk and hopeful for a future at peace, they adapted well to a rapidly changing world.

This book provides a full commentary on home life during those wartime years. Drawing on an unrivalled collection of contemporary women's magazines, the authors have extracted features, fashion tips, morale-boosting stories, mottoes and recipes to present a panoramic view of women's shifting roles.

Emotional reactions, the practicalities of working and maintaining a home, relationships with Allied troops and, of course, love, leisure and fashion are all included, together with advertisements and readers' letters from the war years. As never before, the portrait that emerges of women in wartime is one of immense courage, good humour and ingenuity.

ISBN 0 356 12887 3
Price (in UK only) **£9.99**

BLITZ: THE CIVILIAN WAR 1940–45
by Jane Waller and Michael Vaughan-Rees

In 1940, no one knew if Britain could survive a blitzkrieg. Would the bombs destroy the fabric of society – the civilian morale upon which the war effort depended – along with the bricks and mortar? And would the civil defence preparations be adequate?

This extraordinary book uses first-hand accounts, published memoirs and contemporary diaries and letters to create a vivid picture of the chaos and fear, and bears witness to the courage, spirit and good humour of those who experienced the BLITZ.

'When that first siren went, we thought we'd had it ... we just sat there waiting for the end of the world.' ODETTE LESLEY

'Our preparations seem to be a mixture of superb organisation and purblind muddle.' MARGARET KENNEDY

'As I write, highly civilized human beings are flying overhead, trying to kill me.' GEORGE ORWELL

ISBN 0 356 18792 6
Price (in UK only) **£8.99**

STATE IMPERFECT by Michael Tintner

Just how bad are things in Britain today? How many people are living in poverty? How many people suffer from cancer, heart disease, mental illness? Why is Britain called the 'dirty man of Europe'? What is the divorce rate? How many murders are committed each year?

  State Imperfect presents a complete, accessible breakdown of the major social problems in modern Britain. Hard facts, the most up-to-date figures and dramatic photographs provide an impartial, illuminating and often surprising picture of all the social ills that plague the nation.

ISBN 0 356 17981 8
Price (in UK only) **£9.99**

WOMEN WITH X APPEAL by Lesley Abdela

How did Edwina Currie feel after she resigned as Junior Minister? How does Clare Short handle the male chauvinists in the House of Commons? How does Shirley Williams see her future in politics?

In WOMEN WITH X APPEAL, women at all levels of political life talk openly about their political convictions, and describe the ups and downs of their careers. They shed light on their adventures with the media, and give their opinions on other politicians. Their frank, illuminating and often amusing insights into the hopes, frustrations and challenges of being a woman in a male-dominated establishment present a rare account of what it's *really* like to be a woman in British politics today.

Lesley Abdela founded the all-party 300 Group to campaign for a larger and more active role for women in politics. She has interviewed over 30 women, from Westminster to the town hall and the European Parliament, for this book, and is well acquainted with many of the subjects.

ISBN 0 356 17184 1
Price (in UK only) **£6.99**

CONVERSATIONS WITH MOTHERS AND DAUGHTERS by Celia Dodd

What is it about the bond between mother and daughter that stirs up such powerful emotions? At best, it's an enviable source of enduring support, at worst it's a flashpoint of tension and disappointment. In conversation with Celia Dodd different generations of women, from teenagers to great-grandmothers, talk frankly and often with great emotion about their personal experiences of the relationship, and the influence it has had on their lives. Abandoned daughters, runaway teenagers, daughters who care for invalid mothers, women who have lived through anorexia, the menopause, or estrangement, share the insights their different experiences have given them.

The impact of the 'New Man', working mothers and the superwoman on the relationship are also assessed. As parental roles blur and women gain greater confidence outside the home, new role models are emerging to inspire generations of daughters to come.

Whether they speak from a Yorkshire mining village, a Glasgow tenement, the home counties, or London's Asian communities, these mothers and daughters all bear witness to the power and influence of the first, and often the most important, relationship in a woman's life.

ISBN 0 356 12891 1
Price (in UK only) **£5.99**

All Optima books are available at your bookshop or news-agent, or can be ordered from the following address:

Optima Books
Cash Sales Department
PO Box 11
Falmouth
Cornwall TR10 9EN

Alternatively you may fax your order to the above address. Fax number: 0326 76423

Payments can be made as follows: Cheque, postal order (payable to Macdonald & Co (Publishers) Ltd) or by credit cards, Visa/Access. *Do not send cash or currency.*

UK customers, please send a cheque or postal order (no currency) and allow 80p for postage and packing for the first book plus 20p for each additional book up to a maximum charge of £2.00.

BFPO customers, please allow 80p for the first book plus 20p for each additional book.

Overseas customers, including Ireland, please allow £1.50 for postage and packing for the first book, £1.00 for the second book and 30p for each additional book.

NAME (Block letters) ....

ADDRESS ....

....

    I enclose my remittance for _____

    I wish to pay by Access/Visa Card

Number | | | | | | | | | | | | | | | | | |

Card expiry date